hot
food

hot food

MURDOCH
B O O K S

Contents

Soups

Prawn gumbo

2 tablespoons olive oil
1 large onion, finely chopped
3 garlic cloves, crushed
1 red capsicum (pepper), chopped
4 rashers bacon, chopped
1½ teaspoons dried thyme
2 teaspoons dried oregano
1 teaspoon paprika
½ teaspoon cayenne pepper
60 ml (¼ cup) sherry
1 litre (4 cups) fish stock
100 g (½ cup) long-grain rice
2 bay leaves
400 g (14 oz) can chopped tomatoes
150 g (5½ oz) okra, thinly sliced
850 g (1 lb 14 oz) medium raw
   prawns (shrimp), peeled and
   deveined
3 tablespoons finely chopped flat-leaf
   (Italian) parsley

Heat the oil in a large saucepan over low heat. Cook the onion, garlic, capsicum and bacon for 5 minutes, or until soft. Stir in the herbs and spices. Season. Add the sherry and cook until evaporated, then add the stock and 500 ml (2 cups) water. Bring to the boil. Add the rice and bay leaves, reduce the heat and simmer, covered, for 20 minutes.

Add the tomato and okra. Simmer, covered, for 20–25 minutes. Stir in the prawns and parsley and simmer for 5 minutes, or until the prawns are cooked through.

Serves 4

Pumpkin and carrot soup

40 g (1½ oz) butter
1 large onion, chopped
2 garlic cloves, crushed
500 g (1 lb 2 oz) carrots, sliced
125 ml (½ cup) orange juice
750 g (1 lb 10 oz) butternut pumpkin
  (squash), peeled and roughly
  chopped
1.5 litres (6 cups) chicken stock
1 tablespoon snipped chives
herb scones or herb bread, to serve

Melt the butter in a large saucepan over medium heat and cook the onion for 5 minutes, or until soft and starting to brown. Add the garlic and carrot and cook for another 5 minutes, or until starting to soften. Pour in the orange juice and bring to the boil over high heat. Add the pumpkin, stock and 500 ml (2 cups) water and return to the boil. Reduce the heat and simmer for 30 minutes, or until the carrot and pumpkin are soft.

Blend the soup in batches in a blender until smooth — add a little more stock if you prefer the soup to be a thinner consistency.

Return to the cleaned pan and reheat. Season to taste with salt and freshly ground pepper. Divide the soup among serving bowls and garnish with the chives. Serve with herb scones or bread.

Serves 4–6

Grilled Italian sausage and vegetable soup

500 g (1 lb 2 oz) Italian pork sausages
200 g (7 oz) piece speck (see Note)
1 tablespoon olive oil
1 large onion, chopped
3 garlic cloves, crushed
1 celery stalk, cut in half and sliced
1 large carrot, cut into 1 cm (1/2 inch)
  cubes
bouquet garni (1 parsley sprig,
  1 oregano sprig, 2 bay leaves)
1 small red chilli, halved lengthways
400 g (14 oz) can chopped tomatoes
1.75 litres (7 cups) chicken stock
300 g (10 1/2 oz) Brussels sprouts, cut
  in half from top to base
300 g (10 1/2 oz) green beans, cut into
  3 cm (1 1/4 inch) lengths
300 g (10 1/2 oz) shelled broad beans,
  fresh or frozen
2 tablespoons chopped flat-leaf
  (Italian) parsley

Grill (broil) the sausages under a hot grill (broiler) for 8–10 minutes, turning occasionally, or until brown. Remove and cut into 3 cm (1 1/4 inch) lengths. Trim and reserve the fat from the speck, then dice the speck.

Heat the oil in a large saucepan over medium heat. Add the speck and reserved speck fat and cook for 2–3 minutes, or until golden. Add the onion, garlic, celery and carrot, reduce the heat to low and cook for 6–8 minutes, or until softened. Discard the remains of the speck fat.

Stir in the sausages, bouquet garni, chilli and chopped tomato and cook for 5 minutes. Add the stock, bring to the boil, then reduce the heat and simmer for 1 hour. Add the Brussels sprouts, green beans and broad beans and simmer for 30 minutes. Discard the bouquet garni, then stir in the parsley. Season to taste. Divide among four bowls and serve.

Serves 4

Note: Speck is cured smoked ham or pork belly. It has a strong taste and is usually cut into small pieces and used as a flavour base.

Leek and potato soup

50 g (1³/₄ oz) butter
1 onion, finely chopped
3 leeks, white part only, sliced
1 celery stalk, finely chopped
1 garlic clove, finely chopped
200 g (7 oz) potatoes, chopped
750 ml (3 cups) chicken stock
220 ml (7¹/₂ fl oz) cream
2 tablespoons chopped chives

Melt the butter in a large saucepan and add the onion, leek, celery and garlic. Cover the pan and cook, stirring occasionally, over low heat for 15 minutes, or until the vegetables are softened but not browned. Add the potato and stock and bring to the boil.

Reduce the heat and leave to simmer, covered, for 20 minutes. Allow the soup to cool a little before puréeing in a blender or food processor. Return to the cleaned saucepan.

Bring the soup gently back to the boil and stir in the cream. Season with salt and white pepper and reheat without boiling. Serve hot or well chilled, garnished with chives.

Serves 6

Tomato and bread soup

750 g (1 lb 10 oz) vine-ripened
  tomatoes
1 loaf (450 g/1 lb) day-old crusty
  Italian bread
1 tablespoon olive oil
3 garlic cloves, crushed
1 tablespoon tomato paste (purée)
1.25 litres (5 cups) hot vegetable
  stock
4 tablespoons torn basil leaves
2–3 tablespoons extra virgin olive oil,
  plus extra, to serve

Score a cross in the base of each tomato. Place in a bowl of boiling water for 1 minute, then plunge into cold water and peel the skin away from the cross. Cut the tomatoes in half and scoop out the seeds with a teaspoon. Chop the tomato flesh.

Remove most of the crust from the bread and discard. Cut the bread into 3 cm (1¼ inch) pieces.

Heat the oil in a large saucepan. Add the garlic, tomato and tomato paste, then reduce the heat and simmer, stirring occasionally, for 15 minutes until thickened. Add the stock and bring to the boil, stirring for 2 minutes. Reduce the heat to medium, add the bread pieces and cook, stirring, for 5 minutes, or until the bread softens and absorbs most of the liquid. Add more stock or water if necessary.

Stir in the torn basil leaves and extra virgin olive oil, and leave for 5 minutes so the flavours have time to develop. Drizzle with a little of the extra oil.

Serves 4

Note: This soup is popular in Italy in the summer months when tomatoes are at their tastiest, and as a way of using up leftover bread. In Italy, the soup is called *Pappa al pomodoro*.

Asparagus soup with Parmesan crisps

725 g (1 lb 9½ oz) fresh asparagus, trimmed
1 tablespoon vegetable oil
30 g (1 oz) butter
1 large red onion, finely chopped
1 large leek, thinly sliced
2 large potatoes, cut into 1 cm (½ inch) cubes
1.25 litres (5 cups) chicken stock
80 ml (⅓ cup) cream
90 g (⅓ cup) sour cream
1 tablespoon snipped chives
60 g (⅔ cup) grated Parmesan

Roughly chop 650 g (1 lb 7 oz) of the asparagus and cut the rest into 6 cm (2½ inch) pieces. Heat the oil and butter in a large saucepan over medium heat and cook the onion and leek for 5 minutes, or until soft. Add the potato, chopped asparagus and chicken stock and bring to the boil over high heat. Reduce the heat and simmer for 8 minutes, or until the vegetables are tender. Blanch the remaining asparagus in a saucepan of boiling water.

Cool the soup, then purée it. Return to the pan and stir in the cream for 1–2 minutes, or until heated through. Season. Garnish with sour cream, the blanched asparagus and chives.

To make the Parmesan crisps, preheat the oven to 190°C (375°F/Gas 5). Line three baking trays with baking paper and place four 9 cm (3½ inch) egg rings on each tray. Sprinkle 5 g (⅛ oz) of the Parmesan into each ring in a thin layer. For a lacy edge, remove the rings. Bake for 5 minutes, or until melted and just golden brown. Allow to cool and serve with the soup.

Serves 4

Chicken laksa

Chicken balls
500 g (1 lb 2 oz) minced (ground)
  chicken
1 small red chilli, finely chopped
2 garlic cloves, finely chopped
1/2 small red onion, finely chopped
1 stem lemon grass (white part only),
  finely chopped
2 tablespoons chopped coriander
  (cilantro) leaves

200 g (7 oz) dried rice vermicelli
1 tablespoon peanut oil
75 g (1/4 cup) good-quality laksa paste
1 litre (4 cups) chicken stock
500 ml (2 cups) coconut milk
8 fried tofu puffs, cut in half on the
  diagonal
90 g (1 cup) bean sprouts
2 tablespoons shredded Vietnamese
  mint
3 tablespoons shredded coriander
  (cilantro) leaves
lime wedges, to serve
fish sauce, to serve (optional)

To make the balls, process all the ingredients in a food processor until just combined. Roll tablespoons of mixture into balls with wet hands.

Place the vermicelli in a heatproof bowl, cover with boiling water and soak for 6–7 minutes. Drain well.

Heat the oil in a large saucepan over medium heat. Add the laksa paste and cook for 1–2 minutes, or until aromatic. Add the stock, reduce the heat and simmer for 10 minutes. Add the coconut milk and the chicken balls and simmer for 5 minutes, or until the balls are cooked through.

Divide the vermicelli, tofu puffs and bean sprouts among four serving bowls and ladle the soup over the top, dividing the balls evenly. Garnish with the mint and coriander leaves. Serve with the lime wedges and, if desired, fish sauce.

Serves 4

Ravioli broth with lemon and baby spinach

Stock
1.5 kg (3 lb 5 oz) chicken bones
  (necks, backs, wings)
2 large leeks, chopped
2 large carrots, chopped
2 large celery stalks, chopped
6 lemon thyme sprigs
4 flat-leaf (Italian) parsley sprigs
10 black peppercorns

350 g (12 oz) fresh veal ravioli
2 strips lemon zest (6 cm/2½ inch
  long), white pith removed
150 g (5½ oz) baby English spinach
  leaves, stems removed
½ teaspoon lemon oil
1–2 tablespoons lemon juice
35 g (⅓ cup) shaved Parmesan,
  to garnish

Place the chicken bones in a large pan with 3 litres (12 cups) cold water. Bring to a simmer over medium–low heat (do not boil) for 30 minutes, removing any scum that rises to the surface. Add the remaining stock ingredients and simmer, partially covered, for 3 hours. Strain through a fine sieve and cool. Cover and refrigerate overnight. Remove the layer of fat on the surface.

Place the stock in a large saucepan and bring to the boil. Add the ravioli and zest and cook for 3–5 minutes, or until the ravioli floats to the top and is tender. Stir in the spinach and season. Discard the zest and, just before serving, stir in the lemon oil (to taste) and lemon juice. Garnish with the shaved Parmesan.

Serves 4

Lentil and vegetable soup with spiced yoghurt

2 tablespoons olive oil
1 small leek (white part only), chopped
2 garlic cloves, crushed
2 teaspoons curry powder
1 teaspoon ground cumin
1 teaspoon garam masala
1 litre (4 cups) vegetable stock
1 fresh bay leaf
185 g (1 cup) brown lentils
450 g (1 lb) butternut pumpkin (squash), peeled and cut into 1 cm (1/2 inch) cubes
400 g (14 oz) can chopped tomatoes
2 zucchini (courgettes), cut in half lengthways and sliced
200 g (7 oz) broccoli, cut into small florets
1 small carrot, diced
80 g (1/2 cup) peas
1 tablespoon chopped mint

Spiced yoghurt
250 g (1 cup) thick natural yoghurt
1 tablespoon chopped coriander (cilantro) leaves
1 garlic clove, crushed
3 dashes Tabasco sauce

Heat the oil in a saucepan over medium heat. Add the leek and garlic and cook for 4–5 minutes, or until soft and lightly golden. Add the curry powder, cumin and garam masala and cook for 1 minute, or until the spices are fragrant.

Add the stock, bay leaf, lentils and pumpkin. Bring to the boil, then reduce the heat to low and simmer for 10–15 minutes, or until the lentils are tender. Season well.

Add the tomatoes, zucchini, broccoli, carrot and 500 ml (2 cups) water and simmer for 10 minutes, or until the vegetables are tender. Add the peas and simmer for 2–3 minutes.

To make the spiced yoghurt, place the yoghurt, coriander, garlic and Tabasco in a small bowl and stir until combined. Dollop a spoonful of the yoghurt on each serving of soup and garnish with the chopped mint.

Serves 6

Pork congee

300 g (1 1/2 cups) long-grain rice,
thoroughly rinsed
1/2 star anise
2 spring onions (scallions), white part
only
4 x 4 cm (1 1/2 x 1 1/2 inch) piece ginger,
cut into slices
3.5 litres (14 cups) chicken stock
1 tablespoon peanut oil
2 garlic cloves, crushed
1 teaspoon grated ginger, extra
400 g (14 oz) minced (ground) pork
ground white pepper
60 ml (1/4 cup) light soy sauce
sesame oil, to drizzle
6 fried dough sticks (see Note)

Put the rice in a large saucepan
with the star anise, spring onions,
sliced ginger and chicken stock.
Bring to the boil, then reduce the
heat to low and simmer for 1 1/2 hours,
stirring occasionally.

Heat the oil in a frying pan over high
heat. Cook the garlic and grated
ginger for 30 seconds. Add the mince
and cook for 5 minutes, or until
browned, breaking up any lumps with
the back of a spoon.

Remove the star anise, spring onions
and ginger from the soup and discard
them. Add the mince mixture and
simmer for 10 minutes. Season with
white pepper and stir in the soy
sauce. Serve with a drizzle of sesame
oil and the dough sticks.

Serves 4–6

Note: Fried dough sticks are available
at Chinese bakeries and speciality
shops and are best eaten soon after
purchasing. If not, reheat in a 200°C
(400°F/Gas 6) oven for 5 minutes,
then serve.

Zucchini soup

60 g (2¼ oz) butter
2 large leeks (white part only), thinly
  sliced
4 garlic cloves, crushed
1.25 kg (2 lb 12 oz) zucchini
  (courgettes), coarsely grated
1.75 litres (7 cups) chicken stock
⅓ cup (80 ml) cream
bacon and onion bread, to serve
  (optional)

Melt the butter in a saucepan over medium heat. Cook the leek, stirring once or twice, for 2–3 minutes, or until it starts to soften. Reduce the heat to low, add the garlic and cook, covered, stirring once or twice, for 10 minutes, or until the leek is really soft — do not allow it to brown.

Add the zucchini to the pan and cook, uncovered, for 4–5 minutes. Pour in the chicken stock and bring to the boil over high heat. Reduce the heat to medium–low and simmer for 20 minutes, or until soft.

Let the soup cool slightly and blend half in a blender until smooth. Return to the pan, stir in the cream and gently reheat over medium heat until warmed through. Season to taste with salt and freshly ground black pepper. Serve the soup with bacon and onion bread or crusty fresh bread, if desired.

Serves 4

Orange sweet potato soup

40 g (1 1/2 oz) butter
2 onions, chopped
2 garlic cloves, crushed
1 kg (2 lb 4 oz) orange sweet potato,
  peeled and chopped
1 large celery stalk, chopped
1 large green apple, peeled, cored
  and chopped
1 1/2 teaspoons ground cumin
2 litres (8 cups) chicken stock
125 g (1/2 cup) thick natural yoghurt
lavash bread, to serve (optional)

Melt the butter in a large pan over low heat. Add the onion and cook, stirring occasionally, for 10 minutes, or until soft. Add the garlic, sweet potato, celery, apple and 1 teaspoon of the cumin and continue to cook for 5–7 minutes, or until well coated. Add the chicken stock and the remaining cumin and bring to the boil over high heat. Reduce the heat and simmer for 25–30 minutes, or until the sweet potato is very soft.

Cool the soup slightly and blend in batches until smooth. Return to the cleaned pan and gently stir over medium heat until warmed through. Season with salt and freshly ground black pepper. Divide among serving bowls and top each serve with a dollop of yoghurt.

Cut the lavash bread into rectangular strips, brush lightly with oil and place on a baking tray. Bake in a 190°C (375°F/Gas 5) oven for 15–20 minutes, or until crisp and lightly golden. Serve with the soup.

Serves 4–6

Chicken, mushroom and Madeira soup

10 g (1/4 oz) dried porcini mushrooms
25 g (1 oz) butter
1 leek (white part only), thinly sliced
250 g (9 oz) pancetta or bacon, chopped
200 g (7 oz) Swiss brown mushrooms, roughly chopped
300 g (10½ oz) large field mushrooms, roughly chopped
2 tablespoons plain (all-purpose) flour
125 ml (½ cup) Madeira
1.25 litres (5 cups) chicken stock
1 tablespoon olive oil
2 chicken breast fillets (about 200 g/7 oz each)
80 g (1/3 cup) light sour cream
2 teaspoons chopped marjoram, plus whole leaves, to garnish

Soak the porcini in 250 ml (1 cup) boiling water for 20 minutes.

Melt the butter in a large saucepan over medium heat and cook the leek and pancetta for 5 minutes, or until the leek is softened. Add all the mushrooms and the porcini soaking liquid and cook for 10 minutes.

Stir in the flour and cook for 1 minute. Add the Madeira and cook, stirring, for 10 minutes. Stir in the stock, bring to the boil, then reduce the heat and simmer for 45 minutes. Cool slightly.

Heat the oil in a frying pan and cook the chicken fillets for 4–5 minutes each side, or until cooked through. Remove from the pan and thinly slice.

Blend the soup until smooth. Return to the cleaned saucepan, add the sour cream and chopped marjoram and stir over medium heat for about 1–2 minutes to warm through. Season. Top with the chicken and garnish with marjoram.

Serves 4

Long and short noodle soup

300 g (10½ oz) minced (ground) pork
4 spring onions (scallions), sliced
3 garlic cloves, roughly chopped
2 teaspoons grated ginger
2 teaspoons cornflour (cornstarch)
125 ml (½ cup) light soy sauce
3 tablespoons Chinese rice wine
30 won ton wrappers
3 litres (12 cups) ready-made Chinese
   chicken broth, or home-made or
   ready-made chicken stock
200 g (7 oz) dried flat egg noodles
2 spring onions (scallions), extra,
   sliced on the diagonal
1 teaspoon sesame oil

Put the minced pork, spring onion, garlic, grated ginger, cornflour, 1½ tablespoons of the soy sauce and 1 tablespoon of the rice wine in a food processor and process until well combined. Place 2 teaspoons of the mixture in the centre of a won ton wrapper and lightly brush the edges with water. Lift the sides up tightly and pinch around the filling to form a pouch. Repeat this process to make 30 won tons.

Place the chicken broth in a large saucepan and bring to a simmer over medium–high heat. Stir in the remaining soy sauce and rice wine.

Meanwhile, bring a large pan of water to the boil. Reduce the heat, add the won tons and simmer for 1 minute, or until they float to the surface and are cooked through, then remove with a slotted spoon. Return the water to the boil, add the egg noodles and cook for 3 minutes, or until tender. Drain and add to the chicken broth along with the cooked won tons. Simmer for 2 minutes, or until heated through.

Divide the broth, noodles and won tons among six large serving bowls, sprinkle with extra spring onion and drizzle each with a little sesame oil.

Serves 6

Chickpea soup with spiced pitta bread

1 tablespoon olive oil
1 large onion, chopped
5 garlic cloves, chopped
1 large carrot, chopped
1 bay leaf
2 celery stalks, chopped
1 teaspoon ground cumin
1/2 teaspoon ground cinnamon
3 x 425 g (15 oz) cans chickpeas,
   drained and rinsed
1.25 litres (5 cups) chicken stock
1 tablespoon finely chopped flat-leaf
   (Italian) parsley, plus extra,
   to garnish
1 tablespoon finely chopped
   coriander (cilantro) leaves
2 tablespoons lemon juice
extra virgin olive oil, to drizzle

Spiced pitta bread
40 g (1 1/2 oz) butter
2 tablespoons olive oil
2 garlic cloves, crushed
1/8 teaspoon ground cumin
1/8 teaspoon ground cinnamon
1/8 teaspoon cayenne pepper
1/2 teaspoon sea salt
4 small pitta breads, split

Heat the oil in a large saucepan and cook the onion over medium heat for 3–4 minutes, or until soft. Add the garlic, carrot, bay leaf and celery and cook for 4 minutes, or until the vegetables start to caramelize.

Stir in the cumin and cinnamon and cook for 1 minute. Add the chickpeas, stock and 1 litre (4 cups) water and bring to the boil. Reduce the heat and simmer for 1 hour. Allow to cool.

Remove the bay leaf and purée the soup. Return to the cleaned pan and stir over medium heat until warmed. Stir in the herbs and lemon juice. Season. Drizzle with oil and garnish with parsley.

To make the spiced pitta bread, melt the butter and oil in a saucepan over medium heat. Add the garlic, spices and salt and cook for 1 minute. Place the pitta (smooth side up) on a lined tray and grill (broil) for 1–2 minutes, or until golden. Turn and brush with the spiced butter. Grill until golden and serve with the soup.

Serves 4–6

Creamy chicken and corn soup

20 g (³/₄ oz) butter
1 tablespoon olive oil
500 g (1 lb 2 oz) chicken thigh fillets,
    trimmed and thinly sliced
2 garlic cloves, chopped
1 leek, chopped
1 large celery stalk, chopped
1 bay leaf
½ teaspoon thyme
1 litre (4 cups) chicken stock
60 ml (¼ cup) sherry
550 g (1 lb 4 oz) corn kernels (fresh,
    canned or frozen)
1 large floury potato (russet), cut into
    1 cm (½ inch) cubes
185 ml (³/₄ cup) cream, plus extra,
    to drizzle
chives, to garnish

Melt the butter and oil in a large saucepan over high heat. Cook the chicken in batches for 3 minutes, or until lightly golden and just cooked through. Place in a bowl, cover and refrigerate until needed.

Reduce the heat to medium and stir in the garlic, leek, celery, bay leaf and thyme. Cook for 2 minutes, or until the leek softens — do not allow the garlic to burn. Add the stock, sherry and 500 ml (2 cups) water and stir, scraping up any sediment stuck to the bottom of the pan. Add the corn and potato and bring to the boil. Reduce the heat and simmer for 1 hour, skimming any scum off the surface. Cool slightly.

Remove the bay leaf and purée the soup. Return to the cleaned pan, add the cream and chicken and stir over medium–low heat for 2–3 minutes, or until heated through — do not boil. Season. Drizzle with extra cream and garnish with chives. If desired, serve with crusty bread.

Serves 4–6

Duck, shiitake mushrooms and rice noodle broth

3 dried shiitake mushrooms
1 Chinese roast duck (1.5 kg/3 lb 5 oz)
500 ml (2 cups) chicken stock
2 tablespoons light soy sauce
1 tablespoon Chinese rice wine
2 teaspoons sugar
400 g (14 oz) fresh flat rice noodles
2 tablespoons oil
3 spring onions (scallions), thinly
   sliced
1 teaspoon finely chopped ginger
400 g (14 oz) bok choy (pak choi),
   trimmed and leaves separated
¼ teaspoon sesame oil

Place the shiitake mushrooms in a heatproof bowl, cover with 250 ml (1 cup) boiling water and soak for 20 minutes. Drain, reserving the liquid and squeezing the excess liquid from the mushrooms. Discard the woody stems and thinly slice the caps.

Remove the skin and flesh from the roast duck. Discard the fat and carcass. Finely slice the duck meat and the skin.

Place the chicken stock, soy sauce, rice wine, sugar and the reserved mushroom liquid in a saucepan over medium heat. Bring to a simmer and cook for 5 minutes. Meanwhile, place the rice noodles in a heatproof bowl, cover with boiling water and soak briefly. Gently separate the noodles with your hands and drain well. Divide evenly among large soup bowls.

Heat the oil in a wok over high heat. Add the spring onion, ginger and shiitake mushrooms and cook for several seconds. Transfer to the broth with the bok choy and duck meat and simmer for 1 minute, or until the duck has warmed through and the bok choy has wilted. Ladle the soup over the noodles and drizzle sesame oil on each serving. Serve immediately.

Serves 4–6

Avgolemono with chicken

1 carrot, chopped
1 large leek, chopped
2 bay leaves
2 chicken breast fillets
2 litres (8 cups) chicken stock
75 g (1/3 cup) short-grain rice
3 eggs, separated
80 ml (1/3 cup) lemon juice
2 tablespoons chopped parsley
40 g (1 1/2 oz) butter, chopped

Place the carrot, leek, bay leaves, chicken fillets and stock in a large saucepan. Bring to the boil over high heat, then reduce the heat and simmer for 10–15 minutes, or until the chicken is cooked. Strain into a clean saucepan and reserve the chicken.

Add the rice to the liquid, bring to the boil, then reduce the heat and simmer for 15 minutes, or until tender. Cut the chicken into 1 cm (1/2 inch) cubes.

Whisk the egg whites in a clean, dry bowl until firm peaks form. Beat in the yolks until light and creamy, whisk in the lemon juice, then 250 ml (1 cup) of the soup. Remove the soup from the heat and gradually whisk in the egg mixture. Add the chicken and stir over low heat for 2 minutes — do not boil or the egg will scramble. Serve at once with a sprinkle of parsley and dot of butter.

Serves 4

Note: This soup will not stand well — make just before serving.

Spaghetti and meatball soup

150 g (5½ oz) spaghetti, broken into
    8 cm (3 inch) lengths
1.5 litres (6 cups) beef stock
3 teaspoons tomato paste (purée)
400 g (14 oz) can chopped tomatoes
3 tablespoons basil leaves, torn
shaved Parmesan cheese, to garnish

Meatballs
1 tablespoon oil
.1 onion, finely chopped
`2 garlic cloves, crushed
500 g (1 lb 2 oz) lean minced (ground)
    beef
3 tablespoons finely chopped flat-leaf
    (Italian) parsley
3 tablespoons fresh breadcrumbs
2 tablespoons finely grated Parmesan
    cheese
1 egg, lightly beaten

Cook the spaghetti in a large
saucepan of boiling water according
to packet instructions until *al dente*.
Drain. Put the stock and 500 ml
(2 cups) water in a large saucepan
and slowly bring to a simmer.

Meanwhile, to make the meatballs,
heat the oil in a small frying pan over
medium heat and cook the onion for
2–3 minutes, or until soft. Add the
garlic and cook for 30 seconds. Allow
to cool.

Combine the mince, parsley,
breadcrumbs, Parmesan, egg, the
onion mixture, and salt and pepper.
Roll a heaped teaspoon of mixture
into a ball, making 40 balls in total.

Stir the tomato paste and tomato
into the beef stock and simmer for
2–3 minutes. Drop in the meatballs,
return to a simmer and cook for
10 minutes, or until cooked through.
Stir in the spaghetti and basil to warm
through. Season, garnish with shaved
Parmesan and serve.

Serves 4

Cabbage soup

100 g (½ cup) dried haricot beans
125 g (4½ oz) bacon, cubed
40 g (1½ oz) butter
1 carrot, sliced
1 onion, chopped
1 leek, white part only, roughly
  chopped
1 turnip, peeled and chopped
bouquet garni
1.25 litres (5 cups) chicken stock
400 g (14 oz) white cabbage, finely
  shredded

Soak the beans overnight in cold water. Drain, put in a saucepan and cover with cold water. Bring to the boil and simmer for 5 minutes, then drain. Put the bacon in the same saucepan, cover with water and simmer for 5 minutes. Drain and pat dry with paper towels.

Melt the butter in a large heavy-based saucepan, add the bacon and cook for 5 minutes, without browning. Add the beans, carrot, onion, leek and turnip and cook for 5 minutes. Add the bouquet garni and chicken stock and bring to the boil. Cover and simmer for 30 minutes. Add the cabbage, uncover and simmer for 30 minutes, or until the beans are tender. Remove the bouquet garni before serving and season to taste.

Serves 4

Spicy seafood and roasted corn soup

2 corn cobs (700 g/1 lb 9 oz)
1 tablespoon olive oil
1 red onion, finely chopped
1 small red chilli, finely chopped
$\frac{1}{2}$ teaspoon ground allspice
4 vine-ripened tomatoes, peeled and
finely diced
1.5 litres (6 cups) fish stock or light
chicken stock
300 g ($10\frac{1}{2}$ oz) boneless firm white
fish fillets (ling or perch), diced
200 g (7 oz) fresh crab meat
200 g (7 oz) peeled raw prawns
(shrimp), roughly chopped
1 tablespoon lime juice

Quesadillas
4 flour tortillas (19 cm/$7\frac{1}{2}$ inch)
85 g ($\frac{2}{3}$ cup) grated Cheddar cheese
4 tablespoons coriander (cilantro)
leaves
2 tablespoons olive oil

Preheat the oven to 200°C (400°F/ Gas 6). Peel back the husks on the corn cobs (making sure they stay intact at the base) and remove the silks. Fold the husks back over the corn, place in a baking dish and bake for 1 hour, or until the corn is tender.

Heat the oil in a large saucepan over medium heat. Add the onion and cook until soft. Add the chilli and allspice and cook for 1 minute, then add the tomato and stock and bring to the boil. Reduce the heat and simmer, covered, for 45 minutes.

Slice off the kernels from the corn cobs with a sharp knife, add to the soup and simmer, uncovered, for 15 minutes. Add the fish, crab and prawn meat to the soup and simmer for 5 minutes, or until the seafood is cooked. Stir in the lime juice and serve with the quesadillas, if desired.

To make the quesadillas, top one tortilla with half the cheese and half the coriander. Season, then top with another tortilla. Heat 1 tablespoon of the oil in a frying pan and cook the quesadilla for 30 seconds on each side, or until the cheese just begins to melt. Repeat to make the other quesadilla. Cut into wedges.

Serves 4

Vietnamese beef soup

400 g (14 oz) rump steak, trimmed
1/2 onion
1 1/2 tablespoons fish sauce
1 star anise
1 cinnamon stick
pinch ground white pepper
1.5 litres (6 cups) beef stock
300 g (10 1/2 oz) fresh thin rice noodles
3 spring onions (scallions), thinly
  sliced
15 g (3/4 cup) Vietnamese mint leaves
90 g (1 cup) bean sprouts
1 small white onion, cut in half and
  thinly sliced
1 small red chilli, thinly sliced on the
  diagonal
lemon wedges, to serve

Wrap the rump steak in plastic wrap and freeze for 40 minutes.

Meanwhile, put the onion, fish sauce, star anise, cinnamon stick, pepper, stock and 500 ml (2 cups) water in a large saucepan. Bring to the boil, then reduce the heat, cover and simmer for 20 minutes. Discard the onion, star anise and cinnamon stick.

Cover the noodles with boiling water and gently separate the strands. Drain and refresh under cold water.

Remove the meat from the freezer and thinly slice it across the grain.

Divide the noodles and spring onion among four deep bowls. Top with the beef, mint, bean sprouts, onion and chilli. Ladle the hot broth over the top and serve with the lemon wedges.

Serves 4

Note: In Vietnam, noodle soups are called *pho* — beef noodle soup, *pho bo*, is one of the most popular.

Minestrone

200 g (1 cup) dried borlotti beans
50 g (1³/₄ oz) lard or butter
1 large onion, finely chopped
1 garlic clove, finely chopped
15 g (³/₄ cup) parsley, finely chopped
2 sage leaves
100 g (3¹/₂ oz) pancetta or bacon,
    cubed
2 celery stalks, halved then sliced
2 carrots, sliced
3 potatoes, peeled but left whole
1 teaspoon tomato paste (purée)
400 g (14 oz) can chopped tomatoes
8 basil leaves
3 litres (12 cups) chicken or vegetable
    stock
2 zucchini (courgettes), sliced
210 g (1¹/₃ cups) shelled peas
115 g (4 oz) runner beans, cut into
    4 cm (1¹/₂ inch) lengths
¹/₄ cabbage, shredded
150 g (5¹/₂ oz) ditalini, avemarie or
    other small pasta
grated Parmesan cheese, to serve

Pesto
2 garlic cloves, crushed
50 g (¹/₃ cup) pine nuts
80 g (1³/₄ cups) firmly packed basil
    leaves
4 tablespoons grated Parmesan
    cheese
150 ml (5 fl oz) extra virgin olive oil

Put the dried borlotti beans in a large bowl, cover with cold water and leave to soak overnight. Drain and rinse under cold water.

Melt the lard in a large saucepan and add the onion, garlic, parsley, sage and pancetta. Cook over low heat, stirring once or twice, for 10 minutes, or until the onion is soft and golden.

Add the celery, carrot and potatoes and cook for 5 minutes. Stir in the tomato paste, tomato, basil and dried beans. Season with plenty of pepper. Add the stock and bring slowly to the boil. Cover and leave to simmer for 2 hours, stirring once or twice.

If the potatoes haven't already broken up, roughly break them up with a fork against the side of the pan. Taste for seasoning and add the zucchini, peas, runner beans, cabbage and pasta. Simmer until the pasta is *al dente*.

Meanwhile, to make the pesto, place the garlic, pine nuts, basil and Parmesan in a food processor and mix to a paste. Alternatively, use a mortar and pestle. Add the oil in a steady stream, mixing continuously. Season to taste. Serve the soup with a dollop of pesto and the Parmesan.

Serves 6

Moroccan lamb, chickpea and coriander soup

165 g (³/₄ cup) dried chickpeas
1 tablespoon olive oil
850 g (1 lb 14 oz) boned lamb leg, cut
  into 1 cm (¹/₂ inch) cubes
1 onion, chopped
2 garlic cloves, crushed
¹/₂ teaspoon ground cinnamon
¹/₂ teaspoon ground turmeric
¹/₂ teaspoon ground ginger
4 tablespoons chopped coriander
  (cilantro) leaves
2 x 400 g (14 oz) cans chopped
  tomatoes
1 litre (4 cups) chicken stock
160 g (²/₃ cup) dried red lentils, rinsed
coriander (cilantro) leaves, to garnish

Soak the chickpeas in cold water overnight. Drain and rinse well.

Heat the oil in a large saucepan over high heat and brown the lamb in batches for 2–3 minutes. Reduce the heat to medium, return the lamb to the pan with the onion and garlic and cook for 5 minutes. Add the spices, season and cook for 2 minutes. Add the coriander, tomato, stock and 500 ml (2 cups) water and bring to the boil over high heat.

Add the lentils and chickpeas and simmer, covered, over low heat for 1¹/₂ hours. Uncover and cook for 30 minutes, or until the lamb is tender and the soup is thick. Season. Garnish with coriander.

Serves 4–6

Poached seafood broth with soba noodles

250 g (9 oz) dried soba noodles
8 raw prawns (shrimp)
1½ tablespoons finely chopped
 ginger
4 spring onions (scallions), cut on the
 diagonal
100 ml (3½ fl oz) light soy sauce
60 ml (¼ cup) mirin
1 teaspoon grated palm sugar or soft
 brown sugar
300 g (10½ oz) boneless salmon fillet,
 skinned and cut into 5 cm (2 inch)
 strips
300 g (10½ oz) boneless white fish
 fillet, skinned and cut into 5 cm
 (2 inch) strips
150 g (5½ oz) cleaned calamari hood,
 scored and cut into 3 cm (1¼ inch)
 cubes
50 g (1¾ oz) mizuna, roughly
 chopped (see Note)

Cook the noodles in a large saucepan of boiling water for 5 minutes, or until they are tender. Drain and rinse with cold water.

Peel and devein the prawns, reserving the shells and leaving the tails intact. Place the heads and shells in a large saucepan with the ginger, half the spring onion and 1.5 litres (6 cups) water. Bring slowly to the boil and boil for 5 minutes. Strain and discard the prawn heads, shells and spring onion. Return the stock to the pan. Add the soy sauce, mirin and palm sugar to the stock. Heat and stir to dissolve the sugar.

Add the seafood to the pan and poach over low heat for 2–3 minutes, or until it is just cooked. Add the remaining spring onion.

Divide the noodles evenly among four large bowls. Add the seafood, pour on the stock and scatter with the mizuna.

Serves 4

Note: Mizuna is a salad leaf with dark green, feathery and glossy leaves. It has a mild peppery flavour. Young leaves are often used in salads or as a garnish, while older leaves are used in stir-fries or in Japanese cooking.

Red lentil, burghul and mint soup

2 tablespoons olive oil
1 large red onion, finely chopped
2 garlic cloves, crushed
2 tablespoons tomato paste (purée)
2 tomatoes, finely chopped
2 teaspoons paprika
1 teaspoon cayenne pepper
500 g (2 cups) red lentils
50 g (¼ cup) long-grain rice
2.125 litres (8½ cups) chicken stock
45 g (¼ cup) fine burghul (bulgar wheat)
2 tablespoons chopped mint
2 tablespoons chopped flat-leaf (Italian) parsley
90 g (⅓ cup) thick natural yoghurt
¼ preserved lemon, pulp removed, zest washed and julienned

Heat the oil in a saucepan over medium heat. Add the onion and garlic and cook for 2–3 minutes, or until soft. Stir in the tomato paste, tomato and spices and cook for 1 minute.

Add the lentils, rice and chicken stock, then cover and bring to the boil over high heat. Reduce the heat and simmer for 30–35 minutes, or until the rice is cooked.

Stir in the burghul and herbs, then season to taste. Divide the soup among serving bowls, garnish with yoghurt and preserved lemon and serve immediately.

Serves 4–6

Note: This soup will thicken on standing, so if reheating you may need to add more liquid.

Pork and buttered corn ramen soup

200 g (7 oz) Chinese barbecued pork
    (char sui) fillet in one piece
2 small fresh corn cobs (550 g/
    1 lb 4 oz)
200 g (7 oz) dried ramen noodles
2 teaspoons peanut oil
1 teaspoon grated ginger
1.5 litres (6 cups) chicken stock
2 tablespoons mirin
2 spring onions (scallions), sliced on
    the diagonal
20 g ($^3/_4$ oz) unsalted butter
1 spring onion, extra, sliced on
    the diagonal

Cut the pork into thin slices and remove the corn kernels from the cob using a sharp knife.

Bring a large saucepan of water to the boil, add the ramen noodles and cook for 4 minutes, or until tender. Drain, then rinse in cold water.

Heat the oil in a large saucepan over high heat. Stir-fry the grated ginger for 1 minute. Add the chicken stock and mirin and bring to the boil. Reduce the heat and simmer for 8 minutes.

Add the pork slices to the liquid and cook for 5 minutes, then add the corn kernels and spring onion and cook for a further 4–5 minutes, or until the kernels are tender.

Separate the noodles by running them under hot water, then divide among four deep bowls. Ladle on the soup, then place 1 teaspoon butter on each serving. Garnish with the extra spring onion and serve at once.

Serves 4

Note: This soup is traditionally served with the butter on top. However, for a healthier option, it is also quite delicious without the butter.

Oxtail soup with stout and vegetables

2 kg (4 lb 8 oz) oxtails, trimmed
2 tablespoons vegetable oil
2 onions, finely chopped
1 leek, finely chopped
2 carrots, diced
1 celery stalk, diced
2 garlic cloves, crushed
2 bay leaves
2 tablespoons tomato paste (purée)
1 thyme sprig
2 flat-leaf (Italian) parsley sprigs
3.5 litres (14 cups) chicken stock
375 ml (1½ cups) stout
2 tomatoes, seeded and diced
100 g (3½ oz) cauliflower florets
100 g (3½ oz) green beans
100 g (3½ oz) broccoli florets
100 g (3½ oz) asparagus, cut into
   3 cm (1¼ inch) lengths

Preheat the oven to 200°C (400°F/ Gas 6). Place the oxtails in a baking dish and bake for 1 hour, turning occasionally, or until dark golden. Leave to cool.

Heat the oil in a large saucepan over medium heat and cook the onion, leek, carrot and celery for 3–4 minutes, or until soft. Stir in the garlic, bay leaves and tomato paste, then add the oxtails, thyme and parsley.

Add the stock and bring to the boil over high heat. Reduce the heat and simmer for 3 hours, or until the oxtails are tender and the meat falls off the bone. Skim off any scum that rises to the surface. Remove the oxtails and cool slightly.

Take the meat off the bones and discard any fat or sinew. Roughly chop and add to the soup with the stout, tomato and 500 ml (2 cups) water. Add the vegetables and simmer for 5 minutes, or until the vegetables are tender. Season.

Serves 4

Tomato and capsicum soup with polenta and olive sticks

2 tablespoons vegetable oil
2 tablespoons olive oil
2 red onions, finely chopped
2 garlic cloves, crushed
1 tablespoon ground cumin
1/4 teaspoon ground cayenne pepper
2 teaspoons paprika
2 red capsicums (peppers), diced
90 g (1/3 cup) tomato paste (purée)
250 ml (1 cup) dry white wine
2 x 400 g (14 oz) cans chopped
    tomatoes
2 long red chillies, seeded and
    chopped
500 ml (2 cups) chicken or vegetable
    stock
3 tablespoons chopped flat-leaf
    (Italian) parsley
4 tablespoons chopped coriander
    (cilantro) leaves

Polenta and olive sticks
500 ml (2 cups) chicken or vegetable
    stock
185 g (1 1/4 cups) coarse polenta
    (cornmeal)
100 g (3 1/2 oz) pitted Kalamata olives,
    chopped
125 ml (1/2 cup) olive oil, to deep-fry

Heat the oils in a large saucepan over medium heat and cook the onion and garlic for 2–3 minutes, or until soft.

Reduce the heat to low, add the spices and cook for 1–2 minutes. Add the capsicum and cook for 5 minutes. Stir in the tomato paste and wine, simmer for 2 minutes, or until reduced slightly. Add the tomato, chilli, stock and 500 ml (2 cups) water. Season. Simmer for 20 minutes. Purée the soup with the herbs.

To make the polenta and olive sticks, grease a 20 x 30 cm (8 x 12 inch) shallow baking tray. Bring the stock and 500 ml (2 cups) water to the boil in a saucepan. Slowly add the polenta in a fine stream, whisking until smooth. Reduce the heat to low. Cook, stirring constantly, for 15–20 minutes, or until it starts to come away from the side. Stir in the olives, then spoon into the tray, smoothing the surface. Cover and chill for 30 minutes, or until firm. Cut into sticks.

Heat the oil in a large deep frying pan to 190°C (375°F), or until a cube of bread browns in 10 seconds. Cook the sticks in batches on each side for 1–2 minutes, or until crisp. Drain well, and serve with the soup.

Serves 4–6

Chicken and vegetable soup

1.5 kg (3 lb 5 oz) chicken
1 onion
2 large leeks, halved lengthwise and
  well washed
3 large celery stalks
5 black peppercorns
1 bay leaf
2 large carrots, peeled and diced
1 large swede (rutabaga), peeled and
  diced
2 large tomatoes, peeled, seeded and
  finely chopped
165 g ($^3/_4$ cup) barley
1 tablespoon tomato paste (purée)
2 tablespoons finely chopped flat-leaf
  (Italian) parsley

Put the chicken, onion, 1 leek, 1 celery stalk, halved, the peppercorns and bay leaf in a large saucepan and add enough water to cover. Bring to the boil, then reduce the heat and simmer for 1½ hours, skimming any impurities that rise to the surface.

Strain the stock through a fine sieve and return to the cleaned saucepan. Discard the onion, leek, celery, peppercorns and bay leaf, and set the chicken aside. When it is cool enough to handle, discard the fat and bones, then shred the flesh, cover and chill.

Allow the stock to cool, then refrigerate overnight. Skim the fat from the surface, place the stock in a large saucepan and bring to the boil. Dice the remaining leek and celery and add to the soup with the carrot, swede, tomato, barley and tomato paste. Simmer for 45–50 minutes, or until the vegetables are cooked and the barley is tender. Stir in the parsley and shredded chicken. Simmer until warmed through and season.

Serves 4–6

French onion soup

50 g (1¾ oz) butter
750 g (1 lb 10 oz) onions, finely sliced
2 garlic cloves, finely chopped
45 g (⅓ cup) plain (all-purpose) flour
2 litres (8 cups) beef or chicken stock
250 ml (1 cup) white wine
1 bay leaf
2 thyme sprigs
12 slices stale baguette
100 g (3½ oz) Gruyère cheese, finely grated

Melt the butter in a heavy-based saucepan and add the onion. Cook over low heat, stirring occasionally, for 25 minutes, or until the onion is deep golden brown and beginning to caramelize.

Add the garlic and flour and stir continuously for 2 minutes. Gradually blend in the stock and the wine, stirring all the time, and bring to the boil. Add the bay leaf and thyme and season. Cover the pan and simmer for 25 minutes. Remove the bay leaf and thyme and check the seasoning. Preheat the grill (broiler).

Toast the baguette slices, then divide among six warmed soup bowls and ladle the soup over the top. Sprinkle with the grated cheese and grill (broil) until the cheese melts and turns light golden brown. Serve immediately.

Serves 6

Pea and ham soup

500 g (2¼ cups) yellow or green split
  peas
1½ tablespoons olive oil
2 onions, chopped
1 carrot, diced
3 celery stalks, finely chopped
1 kg (2 lb 4 oz) ham bones or a
  smoked ham hock, chopped (see
  Notes)
1 bay leaf
2 thyme sprigs
lemon juice, to taste (optional)

Place the split peas in a large bowl,
cover with cold water and soak for
6 hours. Drain well.

Heat the oil in a large saucepan, add
the onion, carrot and celery and cook
over low heat for 6–7 minutes, or until
the vegetables are soft but not brown.

Add the peas, ham bones, bay leaf,
thyme and 2.5 litres (10 cups) cold
water and bring to the boil. Reduce
the heat and simmer, stirring
occasionally, for 2 hours, or until the
peas are tender, removing any scum
that rises to the surface. Remove the
bay leaf and thyme and discard them.

Remove the ham bones from the
soup, cool slightly, then remove the
meat from the bones and discard the
bones. Return the ham to the soup
and reheat. Season to taste with
pepper and lemon juice, if desired.

Serves 6–8

Notes: Ask your butcher to chop the
ham bones for you.
For a smoother texture, the soup can
be cooled and processed once the
ham bones have been removed.
Return the meat to the puréed soup.

Watercress soup

30 g (1 oz) butter
1 onion, finely chopped
250 g (9 oz) potatoes, diced
625 ml (2½ cups) chicken stock
1 kg (2 lb 4 oz) watercress, trimmed
  and chopped
125 ml (½ cup) cream
125 ml (½ cup) milk
freshly grated nutmeg
2 tablespoons chopped chives

Melt the butter in a large saucepan and add the onion. Cover the pan and cook over low heat until the onion is softened but not brown. Add the potato and chicken stock and simmer for 12 minutes, or until the potato is tender. Add the watercress and cook for 1 minute.

Remove from the heat and leave the soup to cool a little before pouring into a blender or food processor. Blend until smooth and return to the cleaned saucepan.

Bring the soup gently back to the boil and stir in the cream and milk. Season with nutmeg, salt and pepper and reheat without boiling. Serve garnished with chives.

Serves 4

Spicy tomato soup with chorizo

500 g (1 lb 2 oz) chorizo sausage
2 tablespoons olive oil
3 onions, halved and sliced
3 garlic cloves, thinly sliced
½ teaspoon ground cumin
1 teaspoon paprika
1–2 small red chillies, seeded and
   finely chopped
1.5 litres (6 cups) chicken stock
2 x 400 g (14 oz) cans chopped
   tomatoes
4 tablespoons chopped flat-leaf
   (Italian) parsley

Fill a large deep frying pan with about 3 cm (1¼ inch) cold water. Add the chorizo sausage, then bring to the boil over high heat. Reduce the heat and simmer, turning occasionally, for 15 minutes, or until the water evaporates, then continue to cook in any fat left in the pan for 3–4 minutes, or until the chorizo is lightly browned. Allow to cool slightly and break into bite-size pieces.

Heat the oil in a large saucepan over medium heat and cook the onion and garlic for 5–6 minutes, or until soft. Stir in the cumin and paprika, chilli, chicken stock, tomato and half the parsley. Bring to the boil, add the chorizo, then reduce the heat and simmer for 20 minutes. Stir in the remaining parsley and serve.

Serves 4–6

South American black bean soup

330 g (1 ½ cups) black turtle beans
  (black kidney beans)
1 tablespoon vegetable oil
1 onion, finely chopped
1 leek, finely chopped
2 garlic cloves, crushed
2 teaspoons ground cumin
4 rashers bacon, diced
1 litre (4 cups) chicken stock
90 g (⅓ cup) sour cream
1 ½ tablespoons snipped chives

Soak the black beans in a bowl of cold water overnight. Drain.

Heat the oil in a large saucepan over medium heat and cook the onion, leek, garlic and cumin for about 3 minutes, or until soft. Add the bacon and cook for 2–3 minutes, or until lightly browned.

Add the black beans, chicken stock and 500 ml (2 cups) water to the saucepan and bring to the boil over high heat. Reduce the heat and simmer for 1 hour, or until the black beans are tender. Season with salt and freshly ground black pepper.

Cool slightly and blend half the soup in batches in a blender until smooth. Return to the saucepan and stir through the unblended soup. Spoon into bowls, dollop with sour cream and garnish with the chives.

Serves 4

Hot and sour lime soup with beef

1 litre (4 cups) beef stock
2 stems lemon grass, white part only,
   halved
3 garlic cloves, halved
2.5 x 2.5 cm (1 x 1 inch) piece ginger,
   sliced
90 g (1 bunch) coriander (cilantro),
   leaves and stalks separated, leaves
   chopped
4 spring onions (scallions), thinly
   sliced on the diagonal
2 strips of 1.5 x 4 cm ($^5/_8$ x 1$^1/_2$ inch)
   lime zest
2 star anise
3 small red chillies, seeded and finely
   chopped
500 g (1 lb 2 oz) fillet steak, trimmed
2 tablespoons fish sauce
1 tablespoon grated palm sugar or
   soft brown sugar
2 tablespoons lime juice
coriander (cilantro) leaves, extra,
   to garnish

Place the stock, lemon grass, garlic, ginger, coriander stalks, 2 spring onions, the lime zest, star anise, 1 teaspoon of the chopped chilli and 1 litre (4 cups) water in a saucepan. Bring to the boil and simmer, covered, for 25 minutes. Strain and return the liquid to the pan.

Heat a chargrill pan (griddle) until very hot. Brush lightly with olive oil and sear the steak on both sides until browned on the outside, but very rare in the centre.

Reheat the soup, adding the fish sauce and palm sugar. Season with salt and black pepper. Add the lime juice to taste (you may want more than 2 tablespoons) — you should achieve a hot and sour flavour.

Add the remaining spring onion and the chopped coriander leaves to the soup. Slice the beef across the grain into thin strips. Curl the strips into a decorative pattern, then place in the centre of four deep serving bowls. Pour the soup over the beef and garnish with the remaining chilli and a few extra coriander leaves.

Serves 4

Pasta and bean soup

200 g (1 cup) dried borlotti beans
60 ml (¼ cup) olive oil
90 g (3¼ oz) piece pancetta or
bacon, finely diced
1 onion, finely chopped
2 garlic cloves, crushed
1 celery stalk, thinly sliced
1 carrot, diced
1 bay leaf
1 rosemary sprig
1 flat-leaf (Italian) parsley sprig
400 g (14 oz) can chopped tomatoes,
drained
1.625 litres (6½ cups) vegetable stock
2 tablespoons finely chopped flat-leaf
(Italian) parsley
150 g (5½ oz) ditalini or other small
dried pasta
extra virgin olive oil, to drizzle
freshly grated Parmesan cheese,
to serve

Place the borlotti beans in a large bowl, cover with cold water and leave to soak overnight. Drain and rinse.

Heat the oil in a large saucepan, add the pancetta, onion, garlic, celery and carrot and cook over medium heat for 5 minutes, or until golden. Season with black pepper. Add the bay leaf, rosemary, parsley, tomato, stock and beans and bring to the boil. Reduce the heat and simmer for 1½ hours, or until the beans are tender. Add more boiling water if necessary to maintain the liquid level.

Discard the bay leaf, rosemary and parsley sprigs. Scoop out 250 ml (1 cup) of the bean mixture and purée in a food processor or blender. Return to the pan, season with salt and ground black pepper, and add the parsley and pasta. Simmer for 6 minutes, or until the pasta is al dente. Remove from the heat and set aside for 10 minutes. Serve drizzled with extra virgin olive oil and garnished with Parmesan.

Serves 4

Eight treasure noodle soup

10 g (¼ oz) dried shiitake mushrooms
375 g (13 oz) thick fresh egg noodles
1.25 litres (5 cups) good-quality
  chicken stock
60 ml (¼ cup) light soy sauce
2 teaspoons Chinese rice wine
200 g (7 oz) chicken breast fillet, cut
  into 1 cm (½ inch) strips on the
  diagonal
200 g (7 oz) Chinese barbecued pork
  (char sui), cut into 5 mm (¼ inch)
  slices
¼ onion, finely chopped
1 carrot, cut into 1 cm (½ inch) slices
  on the diagonal
125 g (4½ oz) snow peas
  (mangetout), cut in half on the
  diagonal
4 spring onions (scallions), thinly
  sliced

Place the shiitake mushrooms in a heatproof bowl, cover with boiling water and soak for 20 minutes, or until soft. Drain and squeeze out any excess liquid. Discard the woody stems and thinly slice the caps.

Bring a large saucepan of water to the boil and cook the noodles for 1 minute, or until cooked through. Drain, then rinse with cold water. Divide evenly into four deep warmed serving bowls.

Meanwhile, bring the chicken stock to the boil in a large saucepan over high heat. Reduce the heat to medium and add the soy sauce and rice wine, stirring to combine. Simmer for 2 minutes. Add the chicken and pork and cook for another 2 minutes, or until the chicken is cooked through and the pork is heated. Add the onion, carrot, snow peas, shiitake mushrooms and half the spring onion and cook for a further 1 minute, or until the carrot is tender.

Divide the vegetables and meat among the serving bowls and ladle on the hot broth. Garnish each bowl with the remaining spring onion.

Serves 4

Winter lamb shank soup

1 tablespoon olive oil
1.25 kg (2 lb 12 oz) lamb shanks
2 onions, chopped
4 garlic cloves, chopped
250 ml (1 cup) red wine
2 bay leaves
1 tablespoon chopped rosemary
2.5 litres (10 cups) beef stock
425 g (15 oz) can crushed tomatoes
165 g ($^3/_4$ cup) pearl barley, rinsed and
   drained
1 large carrot, diced
1 potato, diced
1 turnip, diced
1 parsnip, diced
2 tablespoons redcurrant jelly
   (optional)

Heat the oil in a large saucepan over high heat. Cook the lamb shanks for 2–3 minutes, or until brown. Remove.

Add the onion to the pan and cook over low heat for 8 minutes, or until soft. Add the garlic and cook for 30 seconds, then add the wine and simmer for 5 minutes.

Add the shanks, bay leaves, half the rosemary and 1.5 litres (6 cups) of the stock to the pan. Season. Bring to the boil over high heat. Reduce the heat and simmer, covered, for 2 hours, or until the meat falls off the bone. Remove the shanks and cool slightly.

Take the meat off the bone and roughly chop. Add to the broth with the tomato, barley, the remaining rosemary and stock and simmer for 30 minutes. Add the vegetables and cook for 1 hour, or until the barley is tender. Remove the bay leaves, then stir in the redcurrant jelly.

Serves 4

Hot and sour prawn soup

1 kg (2 lb 4 oz) medium raw prawns
(shrimp)
1 tablespoon oil
2 tablespoons tom yum paste
2 stems lemon grass (white part only),
  bruised
4 makrut (kaffir) lime leaves
3 small red chillies, thinly sliced
80–100 ml (2½–3½ fl oz) fish sauce
80–100 ml (2½–3½ fl oz) lime juice
2 teaspoons grated palm sugar or
  soft brown sugar
4 spring onions (scallions), thinly
  sliced on the diagonal
4 tablespoons coriander (cilantro)
  leaves

Peel and devein the prawns, leaving
the tails intact. Reserve the prawn
shells and heads. Cover the prawns
and refrigerate.

Heat a wok over high heat, add the
oil and swirl to coat. Cook the prawn
shells and heads over medium heat
for about 8–10 minutes, or until they
turn orange.

Add the tom yum paste and 60 ml
(¼ cup) water and cook for 1 minute,
or until fragrant. Add 2.25 litres
(9 cups) water, bring to the boil,
then reduce the heat and simmer for
20 minutes. Strain into a large bowl,
discarding the prawn shells and
heads. Return the stock to the wok.

Add the prawns, lemon grass, lime
leaves and chilli and simmer for
4–5 minutes, or until the prawns are
cooked. Stir in the fish sauce, lime
juice, sugar, spring onion and
coriander. Discard the lemon grass
and serve immediately.

Serves 4

Goulash soup with dumplings

3 tablespoons olive oil
1 kg (2 lb 4 oz) chuck or round steak,
  cut into 1 cm (1/2 inch) cubes
2 large onions, chopped
3 garlic cloves, crushed
1 green capsicum (pepper), chopped
1 1/2 teaspoons caraway seeds,
  ground
3 tablespoons sweet paprika
1/4 teaspoon ground nutmeg
pinch cayenne pepper
1/2 teaspoon sea salt
400 g (14 oz) can chopped tomatoes
2 litres (8 cups) chicken stock
350 g (12 oz) potatoes, cut into 2 cm
  (3/4 inch) cubes
1 green capsicum (pepper), julienned
2 tablespoons sour cream

Dumplings
1 egg
3 tablespoons finely grated Parmesan
  cheese
75 g (2/3 cup) self-raising flour
pinch cayenne pepper

Heat half the oil in a saucepan and brown the cubed beef in batches for 1–2 minutes. Remove and set aside. Heat the remaining oil in the same pan over low heat. Add the onion, garlic and chopped capsicum and cook for 5–6 minutes, or until softened. Stir in the spices and salt for 1 minute.

Return the beef to the pan and stir to coat. Stir in the tomato and stock and bring to the boil. Reduce the heat to low and simmer, covered, for 1 1/4 hours. Add the potato and cook for 30 minutes. Stir in the julienned capsicum and sour cream. Season.

To make the dumplings, mix together all the ingredients and a pinch of salt with a fork to form a soft dough (add 1–2 tablespoons water if necessary). Turn onto a lightly floured surface and knead for 5 minutes, or until smooth. Roll 1/2 teaspoonfuls of the dough into balls, drop into the simmering soup and cook for 6 minutes, or until cooked. Serve.

Serves 4–6

Pumpkin soup

2 kg (4 lb 8 oz) butternut pumpkin
  (squash)
40 g (1½ oz) butter
2 onions, chopped
½ teaspoon cumin seeds
1 litre (4 cups) chicken stock
1 bay leaf
80 ml (⅓ cup) cream
pinch nutmeg

Peel the pumpkin and chop into small chunks. Melt the butter in a large saucepan, add the onion and cook over low heat for 5–7 minutes, or until soft. Add the cumin seeds and cook for 1 minute, then add the pumpkin pieces, stock and bay leaf. Increase the heat to high and bring to the boil, then reduce the heat and simmer for 20 minutes, or until the pumpkin is soft. Remove the bay leaf and allow the soup to cool slightly.

Blend the soup in batches until it is smooth. Return to the cleaned pan and stir in the cream and nutmeg. Simmer gently until warmed through and season with salt and freshly ground black pepper before serving.

Serves 4

Cauliflower and almond soup with hot cheese rolls

75 g (½ cup) blanched almonds
1 tablespoon olive oil
1 large leek (white part only), chopped
2 garlic cloves, crushed
1 kg (2 lb 4 oz) cauliflower, cut into
  small florets
2 desiree potatoes, (about 370 g/
  13 oz), cut into 1.5 cm (⅝ inch)
  pieces
1.75 litres (7 cups) chicken stock

Cheese rolls
4 round bread rolls
40 g (1½ oz) softened butter
125 g (4½ oz) Cheddar cheese,
  grated
50 g (1¾ oz) Parmesan cheese,
  grated

Preheat the oven to 180°C (350°F/ Gas 4). Place the almonds on a baking tray and toast for 5 minutes, or until golden.

Heat the oil in a large saucepan over medium heat and cook the leek for 2–3 minutes, or until softened. Add the garlic and cook for 30 seconds, then add the cauliflower, potato and stock. Bring to the boil, then reduce the heat and simmer for 15 minutes, or until the vegetables are very tender. Cool for 5 minutes.

Blend the soup with the almonds in batches in a blender until smooth. Season to taste with salt and pepper. Return to the cleaned pan and stir over medium heat until heated through. Serve with the cheese rolls, if desired.

To make the cheese rolls, split the rolls and butter both sides. Combine the grated cheeses and divide evenly among the rolls. Sandwich together and wrap in foil. Bake in the oven for 15–20 minutes, or until the cheese has melted.

Serves 4

Spicy

Lamb korma with saffron rice

2 kg (4 lb 8 oz) leg of lamb, boned,
  trimmed of excess fat, cut into 3 cm
  (1 1/4 inch) cubes
1 onion, chopped
2 teaspoons grated ginger
3 garlic cloves, peeled
2 teaspoons ground coriander
2 teaspoons ground cumin
1 teaspoon cardamom seeds
large pinch cayenne pepper
2 tablespoons ghee or oil
1 onion, sliced, extra
125 g (1/2 cup) thick natural yoghurt
125 ml (1/2 cup) thick (double/heavy)
  cream
1 cinnamon stick
50 g (1/2 cup) ground almonds
toasted slivered almonds, to garnish
coriander (cilantro) leaves, to garnish

Saffron rice
25 g (1 oz) butter
3 bay leaves
400 g (2 cups) basmati rice, washed
  and then soaked in cold water for
  1/2 hour, then drained
1/4 teaspoon saffron threads, soaked
  in 2 tablespoons hot water for
  2 minutes
500 ml (2 cups) boiling vegetable
  stock

Place the lamb in a large bowl. Put the onion, ginger, garlic, spices and 1/2 teaspoon salt in a food processor, and process to a smooth paste. Add the spice mixture to the lamb and mix well to coat. Marinate for 1 hour.

Heat the ghee in a large pan, add the extra onion and cook over low heat for 7 minutes until the onion is soft. Add the lamb in batches and cook, stirring constantly, for 8 minutes until the lamb changes colour. Return all the lamb to the pan and stir in the yoghurt, cream, cinnamon stick and ground almonds. Reduce the heat, cover, and simmer, stirring occasionally, for 50 minutes, or until the meat is tender. Add a little water if the mixture becomes too dry. Season.

To make the saffron rice, melt the butter gently in a large deep frying pan, add the bay leaves and rice and cook, stirring, for 6 minutes, or until all the moisture has evaporated. Add the saffron and soaking liquid to the rice with the stock and 375 ml (1 1/2 cups) boiling water. Season. Bring to the boil, then reduce the heat to low and cook, covered, for 15 minutes, or until the rice is cooked. Serve the korma with the rice and garnish with the almonds and coriander.

Serves 4–6

Chicken with chilli jam and cashews

Chilli jam
10 dried long red chillies
4 tablespoons peanut oil
1 red capsicum (pepper), chopped
1 head (50 g/1¾ oz) garlic, peeled
  and roughly chopped
200 g (7 oz) red Asian shallots,
  chopped
100 g (3½ oz) palm sugar, grated, or
  soft brown sugar
2 tablespoons tamarind purée (see
  Note)

1 tablespoon peanut oil
6 spring onions (scallions), cut into
  3 cm (1¼ inch) lengths
500 g (1 lb 2 oz) chicken breast fillet,
  cut into slices
50 g (⅓ cup) roasted unsalted
  cashews
1 tablespoon fish sauce
15 g (½ cup) Thai basil

To make the chilli jam, soak the chillies in a bowl of boiling water for 15 minutes. Drain, remove the seeds and chop. Put in a food processor, then add the oil, capsicum, garlic and shallots and blend until smooth.

Heat a wok over medium heat and add the chilli mixture. Cook, stirring occasionally, for 15 minutes. Add the sugar and tamarind and simmer for 10 minutes, or until it darkens and reaches a jam-like consistency. Remove from the wok.

Clean and reheat the wok over high heat, add the oil and swirl to coat. Stir-fry the spring onion for 1 minute, then add the chicken and stir-fry for 3–5 minutes, or until golden brown and tender. Stir in the cashews, fish sauce and 4 tablespoons of the chilli jam. Stir-fry for a further 2 minutes, then stir in the basil and serve.

Serves 4

Note: Use a non-stick or stainless steel wok to cook this recipe because the tamarind purée will react with the metal in a regular wok and will taint the dish.

Smoky spiced eggplant

2 large (600 g/1 lb 5 oz) eggplants
  (aubergines)
1 red onion, chopped
1 garlic clove, chopped
2.5 cm (1 inch) piece of ginger,
  chopped
1 green chilli, chopped
100 ml (3½ fl oz) oil
¼ teaspoon chilli powder
½ teaspoon garam masala
2 teaspoons ground cumin
2 teaspoons ground coriander
2 teaspoons salt
½ teaspoon ground black pepper
2 ripe tomatoes, chopped
3–4 tablespoons coriander (cilantro)
  leaves, finely chopped

Using a pair of tongs, scorch the eggplants by holding them over a medium gas flame. Alternatively, heat them under a grill (broiler) or on an electric hotplate. Keep turning them until the skin is blackened on all sides. Set aside until cool, then peel off the charred skin. Roughly chop the flesh. Don't worry if black specks remain on the flesh because they add to the smoky flavour.

Combine the onion, garlic, ginger and chilli in a blender and process until chopped together but not a paste. Alternatively, chop finely with a knife and mix in a bowl.

Heat the oil in a deep heavy-based frying pan over medium heat, add the onion mixture and cook until slightly browned. Add all the spices and the salt and pepper and stir for 1 minute. Add the tomato and simmer until the liquid has reduced.

Put the eggplants in the pan and mash them with a wooden spoon, stirring around with the spices. Simmer for 10 minutes, or until soft. Stir in the coriander leaves and season with salt. Serve with bread as a light meal, or as a cold relish with a main meal, such as an Indian curry.

Serves 4

Stir-fried lamb with mint and chilli

2 tablespoons oil
750 g (1 lb 10 oz) lamb fillet, thinly
  sliced (see Note)
4 garlic cloves, finely chopped
1 small red onion, cut into wedges
2 small red chillies, thinly sliced
80 ml (1/3 cup) oyster sauce
2 1/2 tablespoons fish sauce
1 1/2 teaspoons sugar
25 g (1/2 cup) chopped mint leaves
5 g (1/4 cup) whole mint leaves

Heat a wok over high heat, add
1 tablespoon of the oil and swirl to
coat. Add the lamb and garlic in
batches and stir-fry for 1–2 minutes,
or until the lamb is almost cooked.

Heat the remaining oil in the wok, add
the onion and stir-fry for 2 minutes, or
until the onion is soft.

Return all the lamb to the wok. Stir in
the chilli, oyster sauce, fish sauce,
sugar and the chopped mint leaves
and cook for another 1–2 minutes.

Remove from the heat, fold in the
whole mint leaves and serve with rice.

Serves 4

Note: Make sure you slice the lamb
across the grain — this will help stop
the meat breaking up and shrinking as
it cooks.

Pork vindaloo

1 kg (2 lb 4 oz) leg of pork on the
  bone, trimmed of excess fat
6 cardamom pods
1 teaspoon black peppercorns
4 dried chillies
1 teaspoon cloves
10 cm (4 inch) piece of cinnamon
  stick, roughly broken
1 teaspoon cumin seeds
1/2 teaspoon ground turmeric
1/2 teaspoon coriander seeds
1/4 teaspoon fenugreek seeds
4 tablespoons clear vinegar (see
  Note)
1 tablespoon dark vinegar (see Note)
4 tablespoons oil
2 onions, finely sliced
10 garlic cloves, finely sliced
5 cm (2 inch) piece of ginger, cut into
  matchsticks
3 ripe tomatoes, roughly chopped
4 green chillies, chopped
1 teaspoon jaggery or soft brown
  sugar

Remove the bone from the pork and
cut the meat into 2.5 cm (1 inch)
cubes. Reserve the bone.

Split open the cardamom pods and
remove the seeds. Finely grind the
cardamom seeds and all the other
spices in a spice grinder or mortar
and pestle. In a large bowl, mix the
ground spices together with the
vinegars. Add the pork and mix
thoroughly to coat well. Cover and
marinate in the fridge for 3 hours.

Heat the oil in a casserole dish over
low heat and fry the onion until lightly
browned. Add the garlic, ginger,
tomato and chilli and stir well. Add the
pork, increase the heat to high and fry
for 3–5 minutes, or until browned.
Add 250 ml (1 cup) water and any of
the marinade liquid left in the bowl,
reduce the heat and bring slowly back
to the boil. Add the jaggery and the
pork bone. Cover tightly and simmer
for 1 1/2 hours, stirring occasionally,
until the meat is very tender. Discard
the bone. Season with salt, to taste.

Serves 4

Note: 'Vindaloo' is Portuguese for
'vinegar and garlic'. The clear vinegar
is made from coconut, the dark from
molasses, but white and balsamic
vinegars can be used instead.

Spicy corn puffs

2 corn cobs
3 tablespoons chopped coriander
  (cilantro) leaves
6 spring onions (scallions), finely
  chopped
1 small red chilli, seeded and finely
  chopped
1 large egg
2 teaspoons ground cumin
1/2 teaspoon ground coriander
125 g (1 cup) plain (all-purpose) flour
oil, for deep-frying
sweet chilli sauce, to serve

Cut down the side of the corn with a sharp knife to release the kernels. Roughly chop the kernels, then place them in a large bowl. Holding the cobs over the bowl, scrape down the sides of the cobs with a knife to release any corn juice from the cob into the bowl.

Add the coriander leaves, spring onion, chilli, egg, cumin, ground coriander, 1 teaspoon salt and some cracked black pepper to the bowl and stir well. Add the flour and mix well. The texture of the batter will vary depending on the juiciness of the corn. If the mixture is too dry, add 1 tablespoon water, but no more than that as the batter should be quite dry. Stand for 10 minutes.

Fill a large heavy-based saucepan or deep-fryer one-third full of oil and heat to 180°C (350°F), or until a cube of bread dropped in the oil browns in 15 seconds. Drop slightly heaped teaspoons of the corn batter into the oil and cook for about 1 1/2 minutes, or until puffed and golden. Drain on crumpled paper towels and serve immediately with a bowl of the sweet chilli sauce to dip the puffs into.

Makes about 36

Chilli plum beef

2 tablespoons vegetable oil
600 g (1 lb 5 oz) lean beef fillet, thinly
  sliced across the grain
1 large red onion, cut into wedges
1 red capsicum (pepper), thinly sliced
1½ tablespoons chilli garlic sauce
125 ml (½ cup) good-quality plum
  sauce
1 tablespoon light soy sauce
2 teaspoons rice vinegar
good pinch of finely ground white
  pepper
4 spring onions (scallions), sliced on
  the diagonal

Heat a wok over high heat, then add 1 tablespoon of the oil and swirl to coat the side of the wok. Stir-fry the beef in two batches for 2–3 minutes each batch, or until browned and just cooked. Remove from the wok.

Heat the remaining oil in the wok, add the onion and stir-fry for 1 minute before adding the capsicum and continuing to stir-fry for 2–3 minutes, or until just tender. Add the chilli garlic sauce and stir for 1 minute, then return the meat to the wok and add the plum sauce, soy sauce, rice vinegar, white pepper and most of the spring onion.

Toss everything together for 1 minute, or until the meat is reheated. Sprinkle with the remaining spring onion, then serve with steamed rice or noodles.

Serves 4

Singapore pepper crab

Stir-fry sauce
2 tablespoons dark soy sauce
2 tablespoons oyster sauce
1 tablespoon grated palm sugar or
  soft brown sugar

2 kg (4 lb 8 oz) blue swimmer crabs
1–2 tablespoons peanut oil
150 g (5½ oz) butter
2 tablespoons finely chopped garlic
1 tablespoon finely chopped ginger
1 small red chilli, seeded and finely
  chopped
1½ tablespoons ground black pepper
1 spring onion, green part only, thinly
  sliced on the diagonal

Mix the ingredients for the sauce in a
small bowl or jug and set aside.

Wash the crabs well with a stiff brush.
Pull back the apron and remove the
top shell from each crab (it should
come off easily). Remove the intestine
and the grey feathery gills. Using a
large sharp knife, cut the crab
lengthways through the centre of the
body to form two halves with the legs
attached. Cut each half in half again,
crossways. Crack the thicker part of
the legs with the back of a heavy knife
or crab crackers.

Heat a wok over high heat, add a little
oil and swirl to coat. Add the crab in a
few batches, stir-frying over very high
heat for 4 minutes each batch, or until
the shells turn bright orange, adding
more oil if needed. Remove from the
wok. Reduce the heat to medium–high,
add the butter, garlic, ginger, chilli and
pepper and stir-fry for 30 seconds,
then add the stir-fry sauce and
simmer for 1 minute, or until glossy.

Return the crab to the wok, cover,
stirring every minute for 4 minutes, or
until cooked. Sprinkle with the spring
onion and serve with rice. Provide
bowls of warm water with lemon
slices for rinsing sticky fingers.

Serves 4

Spanish crisp potatoes in spicy tomato sauce

olive oil, for deep-frying
1 kg (2 lb 4 oz) desiree potatoes,
  peeled and cut into 2 cm (³/₄ inch)
  cubes, then rinsed and patted
  completely dry
500 g (1 lb 2 oz) ripe Roma (plum)
  tomatoes
2 tablespoons olive oil, extra
¼ red onion, finely chopped
2 garlic cloves, crushed
3 teaspoons paprika
¼ teaspoon cayenne pepper
1 bay leaf
1 teaspoon sugar
1 tablespoon chopped flat-leaf (Italian)
  parsley

Fill a deep-fryer or large heavy-based saucepan one-third full of oil and heat to 180°C (350°F), or until a cube of bread dropped in the oil browns in 15 seconds. Cook the potato in batches for 10 minutes, or until golden. Drain on crumpled paper towels. Do not discard the oil.

Score a cross in the base of each tomato. Place in a bowl of boiling water for 1 minute, then plunge into cold water and peel the skin away from the cross. Chop the flesh.

Heat the extra olive oil in a saucepan, add the onion and cook over medium heat for 3 minutes, or until soft and golden. Add the garlic, paprika and cayenne and cook for 1–2 minutes. Add the tomato, bay leaf, sugar and 100 ml (3½ fl oz) water and cook, stirring occasionally, for 20 minutes. Cool slightly, remove the bay leaf, then process in a food processor until smooth, adding a little water if needed. Prior to serving, reheat the sauce over low heat. Season well.

Reheat the oil to 180°C (350°F). Recook the potato in batches for 2 minutes, or until crisp. Drain. Place the potatoes on a platter and pour over the sauce. Garnish with parsley.

Serves 6

Chilli beef

60 ml (¼ cup) kecap manis
2½ teaspoons sambal oelek
2 garlic cloves, crushed
½ teaspoon ground coriander
1 tablespoon grated palm sugar or
  soft brown sugar
1 teaspoon sesame oil
400 g (14 oz) beef fillet, partially
  frozen, thinly sliced
1 tablespoon peanut oil
2 tablespoons chopped roasted
  peanuts
3 tablespoons chopped coriander
  (cilantro) leaves

Combine the kecap manis, sambal oelek, garlic, ground coriander, palm sugar, sesame oil and 2 tablespoons water in a large bowl. Add the beef slices and coat well. Cover with plastic wrap and refrigerate for 20 minutes.

Heat a wok over high heat, add the peanut oil and swirl to coat. Add the meat in batches and cook each batch for 2–3 minutes, or until browned.

Arrange the beef on a serving platter, sprinkle with the chopped peanuts and coriander and serve with steamed rice.

Serves 4

Red curry of roast pumpkin, beans and basil

600 g (1 lb 5 oz) peeled and seeded
  pumpkin, cut into 3 cm (1¼ inch)
  cubes
2 tablespoons oil
1 tablespoon ready-made red curry
  paste
400 ml (14 fl oz) coconut cream
200 g (7 oz) green beans, cut into
  3 cm (1¼ inch) lengths
2 makrut (kaffir) lime leaves, crushed
1 tablespoon grated light palm sugar
  or soft brown sugar
1 tablespoon fish sauce
30 g (1 cup) Thai basil leaves, plus
  extra, to garnish
1 tablespoon lime juice

Preheat the oven to 200°C (400°F/
Gas 6). Place the pumpkin in a baking
dish with 1 tablespoon of the oil and
toss to coat. Bake for 20 minutes, or
until tender.

Heat the remaining oil in a saucepan,
add the curry paste and cook, stirring
constantly, breaking up with a fork,
over medium heat for 1–2 minutes.
Add the coconut cream 125 ml
(½ cup) at a time, stirring well with a
wooden spoon between each
addition for a creamy consistency.
Add the pumpkin and any roasting
juices, the beans and lime leaves.
Reduce the heat to low and cook for
5 minutes.

Stir in the palm sugar, fish sauce,
basil and lime juice. Garnish with extra
basil leaves. Serve with rice.

Serves 4

Bombay-style fish

2 garlic cloves, crushed
3 small green chillies, seeded and
    finely chopped
1/2 teaspoon ground turmeric
1/2 teaspoon ground cloves
1/2 teaspoon ground cinnamon
1/2 teaspoon ground cayenne pepper
1 tablespoon tamarind purée
170 ml (2/3 cup) oil
800 g (1 lb 12 oz) pomfret, sole or
    leatherjacket fillets, skinned
310 ml (1 1/4 cups) coconut cream
2 tablespoons chopped coriander
    (cilantro) leaves

Mix together the garlic, chilli, spices, tamarind and 125 ml (1/2 cup) of the oil. Place the fish fillets in a shallow dish and spoon the marinade over them. Turn the fish over, cover and refrigerate for 30 minutes.

Heat the remaining oil in a large heavy-based frying pan and add the fish in batches. Cook for 1 minute on each side. Return all the fish to the pan, then reduce the heat to low and add any remaining marinade and the coconut cream. Season with salt and gently cook for 3–5 minutes, or until the fish is cooked through and flakes easily. If the sauce is too runny, lift out the fish, simmer the sauce for a few minutes, then pour it over the fish. Garnish with the coriander leaves.

Serves 4

Kofta in tomato and yoghurt sauce

Kofta
1 onion, grated
500 g (1 lb 2 oz) minced (ground) lamb
2 cm (³/₄ inch) piece of ginger, grated
3 garlic cloves, finely chopped
2 green chillies, seeded and finely chopped
1/2 teaspoon salt
1 egg

Tomato and yoghurt sauce
2 teaspoons coriander seeds
2 teaspoons cumin seeds
3 tablespoons oil
10 cm (4 inch) piece of cinnamon stick
6 cloves
6 cardamom pods
1 onion, finely chopped
1/2 teaspoon ground turmeric
1 teaspoon paprika
1 teaspoon garam masala
1/2 teaspoon salt
200 g (7 oz) can chopped tomatoes
150 ml (5 fl oz) thick natural yoghurt

coriander (cilantro) leaves, to garnish
naan bread, to serve

To make the kofta, put the onion in a sieve and use a spoon to press out as much of the liquid as possible. Put it in a bowl and mix in the lamb, ginger, garlic, chilli, salt and egg. Divide into 20 equal portions and shape each into a ball. Cover with plastic wrap and refrigerate for 2 hours, or put in the freezer while you make the sauce.

To make the sauce, dry-roast the coriander seeds in a small pan over low heat until aromatic. Remove, then dry-roast the cumin seeds. Grind the roasted spices to a fine powder using a spice grinder or mortar and pestle.

Heat the oil in a heavy-based frying pan over low heat. Add the cinnamon stick, cloves, cardamom pods and onion and fry until the onion is golden. Add all the ground spices and the salt and fry for 30 seconds. Stir in the tomato, then remove from the heat and slowly stir in the yoghurt. Return the pan to the heat, slide in the chilled meatballs and bring to the boil. Simmer, uncovered, for 1 hour, over very low heat, shaking the pan from time to time to prevent the meatballs from sticking (add a little water if the sauce dries out). Remove any whole spices before serving. Garnish with coriander and serve with naan bread.

Serves 4

Easy chicken stir-fry

1 tablespoon cornflour (cornstarch)
2 teaspoons finely chopped ginger
2 garlic cloves, crushed
1 small red chilli, finely chopped
1 teaspoon sesame oil
60 ml (¼ cup) light soy sauce
500 g (1 lb 2 oz) chicken breast fillet,
   thinly sliced
1 tablespoon peanut oil
1 onion, halved and thinly sliced
115 g (4 oz) baby corn, halved on the
   diagonal
425 g (15 oz) baby bok choy (pak
   choi), trimmed and quartered
   lengthwise
2 tablespoons oyster sauce
60 ml (¼ cup) chicken stock

Combine half the cornflour with the ginger, crushed garlic, chilli, sesame oil and 2 tablespoons soy sauce in a large bowl. Add the chicken, toss until well coated and marinate for 10 minutes.

Heat a wok over high heat, add the peanut oil and swirl to coat. Stir-fry the onion for 2 minutes, or until soft and golden. Add the chicken in two batches and stir-fry for 5 minutes, or until almost cooked through. Add the baby corn and stir-fry for a further 2 minutes, then add the bok choy and cook for 2 minutes, or until wilted.

Mix the remaining soy sauce and cornflour with the oyster sauce and chicken stock in a small bowl, add to the wok and stir-fry for 1–2 minutes, or until the sauce has thickened to coating consistency and the chicken is cooked. Serve immediately with steamed rice or noodles.

Serves 4

Jungle curry prawns

Curry paste
10–12 large dried red chillies
1 teaspoon white pepper
4 red Asian shallots, chopped
4 garlic cloves, sliced
1 stem lemon grass, white part only, sliced
1 tablespoon finely chopped galangal
2 small coriander (cilantro) roots, chopped
1 tablespoon finely chopped ginger
1 tablespoon shrimp paste, dry roasted

1 tablespoon peanut oil
1 garlic clove, crushed
1 tablespoon fish sauce
30 g (¼ cup) ground candlenuts
310 ml (1¼ cups) fish stock
1 tablespoon whisky
3 makrut (kaffir) lime leaves, torn
600 g (1 lb 5 oz) raw prawns (shrimp), peeled and deveined, with tails intact
1 small carrot, quartered lengthways and sliced thinly on the diagonal
150 g (5½ oz) snake beans (yard-long beans), cut into 2 cm (¾ inch) lengths
50 g (¼ cup) bamboo shoots
Thai basil leaves, to garnish

To make the curry paste, soak the chillies in boiling water for 15 minutes. Drain and chop. Place in a food processor with the white pepper, shallots, garlic, lemon grass, galangal, coriander roots, ginger, shrimp paste and 1 teaspoon salt and blend until smooth — add a little water, if necessary, to form a paste.

Heat a wok over medium heat, add the oil and swirl to coat the side. Add the garlic and 3 tablespoons of the curry paste and cook, stirring, for 5 minutes. Add the fish sauce, ground candlenuts, fish stock, whisky, lime leaves, prawns, carrot, beans and bamboo shoots. Bring to the boil, then reduce the heat and simmer for 5 minutes, or until the prawns and vegetables are cooked.

Garnish with Thai basil and freshly ground black pepper.

Serves 6

Chilli lamb cutlets

4 garlic cloves, crushed
1 tablespoon grated ginger
1 teaspoon oil
1 teaspoon sambal oelek
2 teaspoons ground coriander
2 teaspoons ground cumin
2 tablespoons soy sauce
2 teaspoons sesame oil
2 tablespoons sweet chilli sauce
2 tablespoons lemon juice
12 lamb cutlets

Combine the garlic, ginger, oil, sambal oelek, coriander, cumin, soy sauce, sesame oil, sweet chilli sauce and lemon juice in a bowl. Season with salt and cracked black pepper.

Place the cutlets in a non-metallic dish and pour on the marinade, coating all sides. Leave to marinate for 20 minutes.

Cook the cutlets on a very hot chargrill pan (griddle) or barbecue for 3 minutes each side, or until cooked to your liking. Serve with steamed rice.

Serves 4

Sweet and sour chickpeas

500 g (2¼ cups) chickpeas
2 tablespoons oil or ghee
2 large red onions, thinly sliced
2 cm (¾ inch) piece of ginger, finely
  chopped
2 teaspoons sugar
2 teaspoons ground coriander
2 teaspoons ground cumin
pinch of chilli powder (optional)
1 teaspoon garam masala
3 tablespoons tamarind purée (see
  Note)
4 ripe tomatoes, chopped
4 tablespoons coriander (cilantro) or
  mint leaves, finely chopped

Soak the chickpeas overnight in 2 litres (8 cups) water. Drain, then put the chickpeas in a large saucepan with 2 litres (8 cups) water. Bring to the boil, spooning off any scum from the surface. Cover and simmer over low heat for 1–1½ hours until soft. It is important they are soft at this stage as they won't soften any more once the sauce has been added. Drain.

Heat the oil in a heavy-based frying pan. Fry the onion until soft and brown, then stir in the ginger. Add the chickpeas, sugar, coriander, cumin, chilli powder, garam masala and a pinch of salt. Stir, then add the tamarind and tomato and simmer for 2–3 minutes. Add 500 ml (2 cups) water, bring to the boil and cook until the sauce has thickened. Stir in the coriander leaves. Serve with Indian bread such as rotis or naan.

Serves 6

Note: Tamarind is a souring agent made from the pods of the tamarind tree. It is sold as a block of pulp (including husks and seeds), as cleaned pulp, or as ready-prepared tamarind purée or concentrate.

Panang beef

Paste
8–10 large dried red chillies
6 red Asian shallots, chopped
6 garlic cloves, chopped
1 teaspoon ground coriander
1 tablespoon ground cumin
1 teaspoon white pepper
2 stems lemon grass, white part only,
    bruised and sliced
1 tablespoon chopped galangal
6 coriander (cilantro) roots
2 teaspoons shrimp paste
2 tablespoons roasted peanuts

1 tablespoon peanut oil
400 ml (14 fl oz) can coconut cream
1 kg (2 lb 4 oz) round or blade steak,
    cut into 1 cm (1/2 inch) slices
400 ml (14 fl oz) can coconut milk
90 g (1/3 cup) crunchy peanut butter
4 makrut (kaffir) lime leaves
3 tablespoons lime juice
2 1/2 tablespoons fish sauce
3–4 tablespoons grated palm sugar or
    soft brown sugar
1 tablespoon chopped roasted
    peanuts, extra, to garnish
Thai basil, to garnish

To make the paste, soak the chillies in a bowl of boiling water for 15 minutes, or until soft. Remove the seeds and chop. Place in a food processor with the shallots, garlic, ground coriander, ground cumin, white pepper, lemon grass, galangal, coriander roots, shrimp paste and peanuts and process until smooth — add a little water if the paste is too thick.

Place the peanut oil and the thick coconut cream from the top of the can (reserve the rest) in a saucepan and cook over medium heat for 10 minutes, or until the oil separates. Add 6–8 tablespoons of the paste and cook, stirring, for 5–8 minutes, or until fragrant.

Add the beef, coconut milk, peanut butter, lime leaves and the reserved coconut cream. Cook for 8 minutes, or until the beef just starts to change colour. Reduce the heat and simmer for 1 hour, or until the beef is tender.

Stir in the lime juice, fish sauce and sugar. Serve garnished with the peanuts and Thai basil.

Serves 4–6

Cajun prawns with salsa

Cajun spice mix
1 tablespoon garlic powder
1 tablespoon onion powder
2 teaspoons dried thyme
2 teaspoons ground white pepper
1 1/2 teaspoons cayenne pepper
1/2 teaspoon dried oregano

Tomato salsa
4 Roma (plum) tomatoes, seeded and
  chopped
1 Lebanese (short) cucumber, peeled,
  seeded, chopped
2 tablespoons finely diced red onion
2 tablespoons chopped coriander
  (cilantro)
1 tablespoon chopped flat-leaf (Italian)
  parsley
1 garlic clove, crushed
2 tablespoons olive oil
1 tablespoon lime juice

1.25 kg (2 lb 12 oz) large raw prawns
  (shrimp)
100 g (3 1/2 oz) butter, melted
60 g (2 1/4 oz) watercress, washed and
  picked over
4 spring onions (scallions), chopped
lemon wedges, to serve

Combine all the ingredients for the Cajun spice mix with 2 teaspoons cracked black pepper.

To make the tomato salsa, combine the tomato, cucumber, onion, coriander and parsley in a bowl. Mix the garlic, oil and lime juice together and season well. Add to the bowl and toss together.

Peel and devein the prawns, leaving the tails intact. Brush the prawns with the butter and sprinkle generously with the spice mix. Cook on a barbecue hotplate or under a hot grill (broiler), turning once, for 2–3 minutes each side, or until a crust forms and the prawns are pink and cooked.

Lay some watercress on serving plates, then spoon the salsa over the leaves. Arrange the prawns on top and sprinkle with some chopped spring onion. Serve with lemon wedges on the side.

Serves 4 (main) or 6 (starter)

Chilli con carne

2 teaspoons ground cumin
1/2 teaspoon ground allspice
1–2 teaspoons chilli powder
1 teaspoon paprika
1 tablespoon vegetable oil
1 large onion, finely chopped
2 garlic cloves, crushed
2 small red chillies, seeded and finely
  chopped
500 g (1 lb 2 oz) minced (ground) beef
400 g (14 oz) can whole tomatoes
2 tablespoons tomato paste (purée)
425 g (15 oz) can red kidney beans,
  drained and rinsed
250 ml (1 cup) beef stock
1 tablespoon chopped oregano
1 teaspoon sugar

Heat a small frying pan over medium heat and dry-fry the cumin, allspice, chilli and paprika for 1 minute, or until fragrant. Remove from the pan.

Heat the oil in a large saucepan over medium heat and cook the onion for 2–3 minutes, or until soft. Add the garlic and chilli and cook for 1 minute. Add the mince and cook over high heat for 4–5 minutes, or until the meat is browned, breaking up any lumps with a fork.

Add the tomatoes, tomato paste, kidney beans, stock, oregano, sugar and spices. Reduce the heat and simmer, stirring occasionally and gently breaking up the tomatoes, for 1 hour, or until reduced and thickened. Season with salt and black pepper. Delicious served with tortillas and guacamole (see page 149).

Serves 4

Thai-style seafood curry with tofu

2 tablespoons soy bean oil or oil
500 g (1 lb 2 oz) firm white fish (ling,
  perch), cut into 2 cm (³/₄ inch) cubes
250 g (9 oz) raw prawns (shrimp),
  peeled and deveined with tails intact
2 x 400 ml (14 oz) cans coconut milk
1 tablespoon Thai red curry paste
4 fresh or 8 dried makrut (kaffir) lime
  leaves
2 tablespoons fish sauce
2 tablespoons finely chopped lemon
  grass (white part only)
2 garlic cloves, crushed
1 tablespoon finely chopped galangal
1 tablespoon shaved palm sugar or
  soft brown sugar
300 g (10½ oz) silken firm tofu, cut
  into 1.5 cm (⁵/₈ inch) cubes
60 g (¼ cup) bamboo shoots,
  julienned
1 large red chilli, finely sliced
2 teaspoons lime juice
spring onions (scallions), chopped,
  to garnish
coriander (cilantro) leaves, chopped,
  to garnish

Heat the oil in a large frying pan or wok. Sear the fish and prawns over medium heat for 1 minute on each side. Remove from the pan.

Place 60 ml (¼ cup) coconut milk and the curry paste in the pan and cook over medium heat for 2 minutes, or until fragrant and the oil separates. Add the remaining coconut milk, lime leaves, fish sauce, lemon grass, garlic, galangal, palm sugar and 1 teaspoon salt. Cook over low heat for 15 minutes.

Add the tofu, bamboo shoots and chilli. Simmer for 3–5 minutes. Return to medium heat, add the seafood and lime juice and cook for 3 minutes, or until the seafood is just cooked. Remove from the heat.

Serve with steamed rice and garnish with the spring onion and coriander.

Serves 4

Potato masala

2 tablespoons oil
1 teaspoon black mustard seeds
10 curry leaves
¼ teaspoon ground turmeric
1 cm (½ inch) piece of ginger, grated
2 green chillies, finely chopped
2 onions, chopped
500 g (1 lb 2 oz) waxy potatoes, cut
    into 2 cm (¾ inch) cubes
1 tablespoon tamarind purée

Heat the oil in a heavy-based frying pan, add the mustard seeds, cover, and when they start to pop add the curry leaves, turmeric, ginger, chilli and onion and cook, uncovered, until the onion is soft.

Add the potato cubes and 250 ml (1 cup) water to the pan, bring to the boil, cover and cook until the potato is tender and almost breaking up. If there is any liquid left in the pan, let it simmer a little, uncovered, until it evaporates. If the potato isn't cooked and there is no liquid left, add a little more and continue to cook. Add the tamarind and season with salt.

Serves 4

Note: This filling is traditionally rolled in dosas — large pancakes made with rice flour — and served for breakfast or as a snack in southern India. However, it also makes an excellent spicy potato side dish.

Madras beef curry

1 tablespoon vegetable oil
2 onions, finely chopped
3 garlic cloves, finely chopped
1 tablespoon grated ginger
4 tablespoons madras curry paste
1 kg (2 lb 4 oz) chuck steak, trimmed
    and cut into 3 cm (1 ¼ inch) cubes
60 g (¼ cup) tomato paste (purée)
250 ml (1 cup) beef stock
6 new potatoes, halved
155 g (1 cup) frozen peas

Preheat the oven to 180°C (350°F/ Gas 4). Heat the oil in a large heavy-based 3 litre (12 cup) flameproof casserole dish. Cook the onion over medium heat for 4–5 minutes. Add the garlic and ginger and cook, stirring for 5 minutes, or until the onion is lightly golden, taking care not to burn it.

Add the curry paste and cook, stirring, for 2 minutes, or until fragrant. Increase the heat to high, add the meat and stir constantly for 2–3 minutes, or until the meat is well coated. Add the tomato paste and stock and stir well.

Bake, covered, for 50 minutes, stirring 2–3 times during cooking, and add a little water if necessary. Reduce the oven to 160°C (315°F/Gas 2–3). Add the potato and cook for 30 minutes, then add the peas and cook for another 10 minutes, or until the potato is tender. Serve hot with steamed jasmine rice.

Serves 6

Cauliflower with mustard

2 teaspoons yellow mustard seeds
2 teaspoons black mustard seeds
1 teaspoon ground turmeric
1 teaspoon tamarind purée
2–3 tablespoons mustard oil or oil
2 garlic cloves, finely chopped
½ onion, finely chopped
600 g (1 lb 5 oz) cauliflower, broken
  into small florets
3 mild green chillies, seeded and
  finely chopped
2 teaspoons kalonji (nigella) seeds

Grind the yellow and black mustard seeds together to a fine powder in a spice grinder or mortar and pestle. Mix with the turmeric, tamarind purée and 100 ml (3½ fl oz) water to form a smooth, quite liquid paste.

Heat 2 tablespoons of the oil in a large heavy-based saucepan over medium heat until almost smoking. Reduce the heat to low, add the garlic and onion and fry until golden. Cook the cauliflower in batches, adding more oil if necessary, and fry until lightly browned, then remove. Add the chilli and fry for 1 minute, or until tinged with brown around the edges.

Return all the cauliflower to the pan, sprinkle it with the mustard mixture and kalonji and stir well. Increase the heat to medium and bring to the boil, even though there's not much sauce. Reduce the heat to low, cover and cook until the cauliflower is nearly tender and the seasoning is dry. Sprinkle a little water on the cauliflower as it cooks to stop it sticking to the pan. If there is still excess liquid when the cauliflower is cooked, simmer with the lid off until it dries out. Season with salt, and remove from the heat. Serve with rice or Indian bread, or as an accompaniment to meat dishes.

Serves 4

Creamy prawn curry

500 g (1 lb 2 oz) tiger prawns (shrimp)
1 1/2 tablespoons lemon juice
3 tablespoons oil
1/2 onion, finely chopped
1/2 teaspoon ground turmeric
5 cm (2 inch) piece of cinnamon stick
4 cloves
7 cardamom pods
5 Indian bay leaves (cassia leaves)
2 cm (3/4 inch) piece of ginger, grated
3 garlic cloves, chopped
1 teaspoon chilli powder
170 ml (2/3 cup) coconut milk

Peel and devein the prawns, leaving the tails intact. Put them in a bowl, add the lemon juice, then toss together and leave for 5 minutes. Rinse the prawns under running cold water and pat dry with paper towels.

Heat the oil in a heavy-based frying pan and fry the onion until lightly browned. Add the turmeric, cinnamon, cloves, cardamom, bay leaves, ginger and garlic and fry for 1 minute. Add the chilli powder, coconut milk and salt, to taste, and slowly bring to the boil. Reduce the heat and simmer for 2 minutes.

Add the prawns, return to the boil, then reduce the heat and simmer for 5 minutes, or until the prawns are cooked through and the sauce is thick. (Care should be taken not to overcook the prawns or they will become rubbery.)

Serves 4

Lamb kofta curry

500 g (1 lb 2 oz) minced (ground)
  lamb
1 onion, finely chopped
1 garlic clove, finely chopped
1 teaspoon grated ginger
1 small chilli, finely chopped
1 teaspoon garam masala
1 teaspoon ground coriander
50 g (½ cup) ground almonds
2 tablespoons chopped coriander
  (cilantro) leaves, to garnish

Sauce
½ tablespoon oil
1 onion, finely chopped
3 tablespoons Korma curry paste
400 g (14 oz) can chopped tomatoes
125 g (½ cup) thick natural yoghurt
1 teaspoon lemon juice

Combine the lamb, onion, garlic, ginger, chilli, garam masala, ground coriander, ground almonds and 1 teaspoon salt in a bowl. Shape into walnut-sized balls with your hands.

Heat a large non-stick frying pan and cook the koftas in batches until brown on both sides — they don't have to be cooked all the way through.

To make the sauce, heat the oil in a saucepan over low heat. Add the onion and cook for 8 minutes, or until soft and golden. Add the curry paste and cook until fragrant. Add the tomatoes and simmer for 5 minutes. Stir in the yoghurt (1 tablespoon at a time) and the lemon juice, stirring until combined.

Place the koftas in the tomato sauce. Cook, covered, over low heat for 20 minutes. Serve over steamed rice and garnish with the coriander.

Serves 4

Beef nachos

2 tablespoons oil
1 onion, chopped
2 garlic cloves, crushed
1 tablespoon ground cumin
3 teaspoons ground coriander
1 teaspoon chilli powder
400 g lean minced (ground) beef
375 g (1½ cups) bottled tomato pasta
    sauce
425 g (15 oz) can refried beans
225 g (8 oz) packet plain corn chips
250 g (2 cups) grated Cheddar
    cheese, at room temperature
150 g (⅔ cup) sour cream
4 spring onions (scallions), green
    parts included, sliced
coriander (cilantro) leaves, to garnish

Guacamole
2 large, ripe avocados
½ small onion, grated
1–2 Jalapeño or serrano chillies,
    seeded and finely chopped (optional)
1 garlic clove, crushed
1 tomato, peeled, seeded and diced
1 tablespoon lime juice
2 tablespoons chopped coriander
    (cilantro) leaves

Preheat the oven to 180°C (350°F/
Gas 4). Heat the oil in a large frying
pan over medium heat and cook the
onion, garlic, cumin, ground coriander
and chilli powder for 2–3 minutes.
Add the mince and cook over high
heat for 3–4 minutes, or until well
browned, breaking up any lumps with
a fork. Stir in the tomato pasta sauce
and refried beans and simmer for
10 minutes until the mixture thickens.

Meanwhile, to make the guacamole,
cut the avocados in half and remove
the stones. Scoop out the flesh, place
in a small bowl and mash roughly with
a fork. Add the onion, chilli (if using),
crushed garlic, tomato, lime juice,
chopped coriander and ¼ teaspoon
salt and stir until well combined.

Divide the corn chips among four
serving plates (ovenproof), arranging
them close together, with a slight
well in the centre. Put in the oven for
10 minutes, or until the corn chips are
hot and golden. Remove and sprinkle
with the grated cheese (the heat from
the chips will melt the cheese). Spoon
equal quantities of the beef mixture
into the well of each pile of chips. Top
with the guacamole and sour cream
and sprinkle with the spring onion.
Garnish with coriander leaves.

Serves 4

Lamb kefta

1 kg (2 lb 4 oz) minced (ground) lamb
1 onion, finely chopped
2 garlic cloves, finely chopped
2 tablespoons finely chopped flat-leaf
  (Italian) parsley
2 tablespoons finely chopped
  coriander (cilantro) leaves
1/2 teaspoon cayenne pepper
1/2 teaspoon ground allspice
1/2 teaspoon ground ginger
1/2 teaspoon ground cardamom
1 teaspoon ground cumin
1 teaspoon paprika

Sauce
2 tablespoons olive oil
1 onion, finely chopped
2 garlic cloves, finely chopped
2 teaspoons ground cumin
1/2 teaspoon ground cinnamon
1 teaspoon paprika
2 x 425 g (15 oz) cans chopped
  tomatoes
2 teaspoons harissa (see Note)
4 tablespoons chopped coriander
  (cilantro) leaves

Preheat the oven to 180°C (350°F/ Gas 4). Lightly grease two baking trays. Place the lamb, onion, garlic, herbs and spices in a bowl and mix together well. Season with salt and pepper. Roll tablespoons of the mixture into balls and place on the trays. Bake for 18–20 minutes, or until browned.

Meanwhile, to make the sauce, heat the oil in a large saucepan, add the onion and cook over medium heat for 5 minutes, or until soft. Add the garlic, cumin, cinnamon and paprika and cook for 1 minute, or until fragrant.

Stir in the tomato and harissa and bring to the boil. Reduce the heat and simmer for 20 minutes, then add the meatballs and simmer for 10 minutes, or until cooked through. Stir in the coriander, season well and serve.

Serves 4

Note: Harissa is a spicy paste made mainly from chillies and is popular in North African cooking. Ready-made harissa can be purchased from delicatessens or speciality shops.

Yellow curry with vegetables

Yellow curry paste
8 small dried red chillies
1 teaspoon black peppercorns
2 teaspoons coriander seeds
2 teaspoons cumin seeds
1 teaspoon ground turmeric
1 1/2 tablespoons chopped galangal
5 garlic cloves, chopped
1 teaspoon grated ginger
5 red Asian shallots, chopped
2 stems lemon grass, white part only, chopped
1 teaspoon shrimp paste
1 teaspoon finely chopped lime zest

2 tablespoons peanut oil
500 ml (2 cups) coconut cream
125 ml (1/2 cup) vegetable stock
150 g (5 1/2 oz) snake beans, cut into 3 cm (1 1/4 inch) lengths
150 g (5 1/2 oz) fresh baby corn
1 slender eggplant (aubergine), cut into 1 cm (1/2 inch) slices
100 g (3 1/2 oz) cauliflower, cut into small florets
2 small zucchini (courgettes), cut into 1 cm (1/2 inch) slices
1 small red capsicum (pepper), cut into 1 cm (1/2 inch) slices
1 1/2 tablespoons fish sauce
1 teaspoon grated palm sugar or soft brown sugar
1 small red chilli, chopped, to garnish
coriander (cilantro) leaves, to garnish

To make the curry paste, soak the chillies in boiling water for 15 minutes. Drain and chop them. Heat a frying pan, add the peppercorns, coriander seeds, cumin seeds and turmeric and dry-fry over medium heat for 3 minutes. Transfer to a mortar or food processor and pound or grind to a fine powder.

Using the mortar and pestle, pound the ground spices, chilli, galangal, garlic, ginger, shallots, lemon grass and shrimp paste until smooth. Stir in the lime zest.

Heat a wok over medium heat, add the oil and swirl to coat the side. Add 2 tablespoons of the curry paste and cook for 1 minute. Add 250 ml (1 cup) of the coconut cream. Cook over medium heat for 10 minutes, or until thick and the oil separates.

Add the chicken stock, the vegetables and remaining coconut cream and cook for 5 minutes, or until the vegetables are tender, but still crisp. Stir in the fish sauce and sugar. Garnish with the chilli and coriander.

Serves 4

Toor dal

500 g (1 lb 2 oz) toor dal (yellow
   lentils)
5 pieces of kokum, each 5 cm (2 inch)
   long (see Note)
2 teaspoons coriander seeds
2 teaspoons cumin seeds
2 tablespoons oil
2 teaspoons black mustard seeds
10 curry leaves
7 cloves
10 cm (4 inch) piece of cinnamon
   stick
5 green chillies, finely chopped
1/2 teaspoon ground turmeric
400 g (14 oz) can chopped tomatoes
20 g (3/4 oz) jaggery or soft brown
   sugar, or 10 g (1/4 oz) molasses
coriander (cilantro) leaves

Soak the lentils in cold water for
2 hours. Rinse the kokum, remove
any stones and put in a bowl with
cold water for a few minutes to soften.
Drain the lentils and place in a heavy-
based pan with 1 litre (4 cups) water
and the kokum. Bring slowly to the
boil, then simmer for 40 minutes, or
until the lentils feel soft when pressed.

Place a small frying pan over low heat
and dry-roast the coriander seeds
until aromatic. Remove and dry-roast
the cumin seeds. Grind the roasted
seeds to a fine powder using a spice
grinder or mortar and pestle.

Heat the oil in a small pan over low
heat. Add the mustard seeds and
allow to pop. Add the curry leaves,
cloves, cinnamon, chilli, turmeric and
the roasted spice mix and cook for
1 minute. Add the tomato and cook
for 2–3 minutes, or until the tomato
is soft and can be broken up easily.
Add the jaggery, then pour the spicy
mixture into the simmering lentils and
cook for 10 minutes. Season with
salt. Garnish with coriander leaves.

Serves 8

Note: Kokum is the sticky dried purple
fruit of the gamboge tree. It imparts
an acid fruity flavour to Indian cuisine.
Sold in Indian food shops.

Spicy

Steamed whole fish with chilli, garlic and lime

1–1.5 kg (2 lb 4 oz–3 lb 5 oz) whole
  snapper, cleaned
1 lime, sliced
red chillies, finely chopped, to garnish
coriander (cilantro) leaves, to garnish
lime wedges, to garnish

Sauce
2 teaspoons tamarind concentrate
5 long red chillies, seeded and
  chopped
6 large garlic cloves, roughly chopped
6 coriander (cilantro) roots and stalks
8 red Asian shallots, chopped
1½ tablespoons oil
2½ tablespoons lime juice
130 g (¾ cup) shaved palm sugar or
  soft brown sugar
3 tablespoons fish sauce

Rinse the fish and pat dry with paper towels. Cut two diagonal slashes through the thickest part of the fish on both sides, to ensure even cooking. Place the lime slices in the fish cavity, cover with plastic wrap and chill until ready to use.

To make the sauce, combine the tamarind with 3 tablespoons water. Blend the chilli, garlic, coriander and shallots in a food processor until finely puréed — add a little water, if needed.

Heat the oil in a saucepan. Add the paste and cook over medium heat for 5 minutes, or until fragrant. Stir in the tamarind, lime juice and palm sugar. Reduce the heat and simmer for 10 minutes, or until thick. Add the fish sauce.

Place the fish on a sheet of baking paper in a large bamboo steamer and cover. Place over a wok of simmering water — ensure the base doesn't touch the water. Cook for 6 minutes per 1 kg (2 lb 4 oz) fish, or until the flesh flakes easily with a fork when tested.

Pour the sauce over the fish and garnish with the chilli, coriander and lime wedges. Serve with rice.

Serves 4–6

Seared scallops with chilli bean paste

500 g (1 lb 2 oz) hokkien (egg) noodles
60 ml (¼ cup) peanut oil
20 scallops, roe and beards removed
1 large onion, cut into thin wedges
3 garlic cloves, crushed
1 tablespoon grated ginger
1 tablespoon chilli bean paste
150 g (5½ oz) choy sum, cut into
  5 cm (2 inch) lengths
60 ml (¼ cup) chicken stock
2 tablespoons light soy sauce
2 tablespoons kecap manis
15 g (½ cup) coriander (cilantro)
  leaves
90 g (1 cup) bean sprouts
1 long red chilli, seeded and finely
  sliced
1 teaspoon sesame oil
1 tablespoon Chinese rice wine

Place the hokkien noodles in a heatproof bowl, cover with boiling water and soak for 1 minute until tender and separated. Drain, rinse under cold water, then drain again.

Heat a wok over high heat, add 2 tablespoons of the peanut oil and swirl to coat the side of the wok. Add the scallops in batches and sear for 20 seconds each side, or until sealed. Remove, then wipe the wok clean. Add the remaining oil and swirl to coat. Stir-fry the onion for 2 minutes, or until softened. Add the garlic and ginger and cook for 30 seconds. Stir in the chilli bean paste and cook for 1 minute, or until fragrant.

Add the choy sum to the wok with the noodles, stock, soy sauce and kecap manis. Stir-fry for 2–3 minutes, or until the choy sum has wilted and the noodles have absorbed most of the liquid. Return the scallops to the wok, add the coriander, bean sprouts, chilli, sesame oil and rice wine, tossing gently until combined.

Serves 4

Beef satay

700 g (1 lb 9 oz) rump steak, cut into
2.5 cm (1 inch) cubes
2 small garlic cloves, crushed
3 teaspoons grated ginger
1 tablespoon fish sauce
2 small red chillies, seeded and
  julienned

Satay sauce
1 tablespoon peanut oil
8 red Asian shallots, finely chopped
8 garlic cloves, crushed
4 small red chillies, finely chopped
1 tablespoon finely chopped ginger
250 g (1 cup) crunchy peanut butter
400 ml (14 fl oz) coconut milk
1 tablespoon soy sauce
60 g (1/3 cup) grated palm sugar or
  soft brown sugar
3 tablespoons fish sauce
1 makrut (kaffir) lime leaf
4 tablespoons lime juice

Combine the steak with the garlic,
ginger and fish sauce and marinate,
covered, in the refrigerator for at least
3 hours. Soak eight wooden skewers
in cold water for 1 hour.

To make the satay sauce, heat the
peanut oil in a saucepan over medium
heat. Cook the shallots, garlic, chilli
and ginger, stirring occasionally, for
5 minutes, or until the shallots are
golden. Reduce the heat to low and
add the peanut butter, coconut milk,
soy sauce, palm sugar, fish sauce,
lime leaf and lime juice. Simmer for
10 minutes, or until thickened, then
remove the lime leaf.

Thread the beef onto the skewers
and cook on a barbecue or chargrill
pan (griddle) over high heat for
6–8 minutes, or until cooked through,
turning halfway through the cooking
time. Top with the satay sauce and
garnish with the julienned chilli. Serve
with rice.

Serves 4

Lamb kebabs

5 garlic cloves, roughly chopped
5 cm (2 inch) piece of ginger, roughly
  chopped
3 green chillies, roughly chopped
1 onion, roughly chopped
3 tablespoons thick natural yoghurt
3 tablespoons coriander (cilantro)
  leaves
1/2 teaspoon ground black pepper
500 g (1 lb 2 oz) minced (ground)
  lamb
red onion rings, to garnish
lemon wedges, to serve

Combine the garlic, ginger, chilli, onion, yoghurt and coriander leaves in a food processor to form a thick smooth paste. If you don't have a processor, chop the vegetables more finely and use a mortar and pestle. Add the pepper, season with salt, then mix in the mince. If you are using a mortar and pestle, mix the mince with the paste in a bowl.

Divide the meat into 16 portions, about 2 tablespoons each. Shape each portion into an oval patty, cover and chill for 20 minutes.

Heat the grill (broiler) to high. Using four metal skewers, thread four meatballs onto each. Grill (broil) for 7 minutes, or until brown on top. Turn over and brown the other side. Check that the meatballs are cooked. Serve with onion rings and lemon wedges.

Serves 4

Stir-fried beef with snake beans and basil

3 bird's eye chillies, seeded and finely
    chopped
3 garlic cloves, crushed
2 tablespoons fish sauce
1 teaspoon grated palm sugar or soft
    brown sugar
2 tablespoons peanut or vegetable oil
400 g (14 oz) lean beef fillet, thinly
    sliced across the grain
150 g (5½ oz) snake beans, sliced
    into 3 cm (1¼ inch) lengths
30 g (1 cup) Thai basil
thinly sliced bird's eye chilli, to garnish

Combine the chilli, garlic, fish sauce, palm sugar and 1 tablespoon of the oil in a large non-metallic bowl. Add the beef, toss well, then cover and marinate in the fridge for 2 hours.

Heat a wok to hot, add 2 teaspoons of the oil and swirl to coat. Stir-fry the beef in two batches over high heat for 2 minutes each batch, or until just browned. Remove from the wok.

Heat the remaining oil in the wok, then add the snake beans and 60 ml (¼ cup) water and cook over high heat for 3–4 minutes, tossing regularly, until tender. Return the beef to the wok with the basil. Cook for a further 1–2 minutes, or until warmed through. Garnish with chilli and serve.

Serves 4

Spicy cellophane noodles with minced pork

200 g (7 oz) minced (ground) pork
1 teaspoon cornflour (cornstarch)
1 1/2 tablespoons light soy sauce
2 tablespoons Chinese rice wine
1 teaspoon sesame oil
150 g (5 1/2 oz) cellophane noodles
   (mung bean vermicelli)
2 tablespoons oil
4 spring onions (scallions), finely
   chopped
1 garlic clove, crushed
1 tablespoon finely chopped ginger
2 teaspoons chilli bean sauce
185 ml (3/4 cup) chicken stock
1/2 teaspoon sugar
2 spring onions (scallions), green part
   only, extra, thinly sliced on the
   diagonal

Combine the mince, cornflour, 1 tablespoon of the soy sauce, 1 tablespoon of the rice wine and 1/2 teaspoon of the sesame oil in a bowl, using a fork or your fingers. Cover with plastic wrap and marinate for 10–15 minutes.

Meanwhile, place the noodles in a heatproof bowl, cover with boiling water and soak for 3–4 minutes, or until softened. Drain well.

Heat a wok over high heat, add the oil and swirl to coat. Cook the spring onion, garlic, ginger and chilli bean sauce for 10 seconds, then add the mince mixture and cook for 2 minutes, stirring to break up any lumps. Stir in the stock, sugar, 1/2 teaspoon salt, and the remaining soy sauce, rice wine and sesame oil.

Add the noodles to the wok and toss to combine. Bring to the boil, then reduce the heat to low and simmer, stirring occasionally, for 7–8 minutes, or until the liquid is almost completely absorbed. Garnish with the extra spring onion and serve.

Serves 4

Rice &
Noodles

Sticky rice pockets

20 dried bamboo leaves
125 ml (½ cup) oil
6 spring onions (scallions), chopped
400 g (14 oz) eggplant (aubergine),
  cut into 1 cm (½ inch) cubes
90 g (3¼ oz) drained water chestnuts,
  chopped
1 tablespoon mushroom soy sauce
3 small red chillies, seeded and finely
  chopped
2 teaspoons sugar
3 tablespoons chopped coriander
  (cilantro) leaves
800 g (4 cups) white glutinous rice,
  washed and well drained
2 tablespoons soy sauce

Soak the bamboo leaves in boiling water for 10 minutes until soft. Drain. Heat half the oil in a wok. Cook the spring onion and eggplant over high heat for 4–5 minutes, or until golden. Stir in the water chestnuts, soy sauce, chilli, sugar and coriander. Cool.

Bring 750 ml (3 cups) water to a simmer. Heat the remaining oil in a saucepan, add the rice and stir for 2 minutes. Stir in 125 ml (½ cup) of the hot water over low heat until it is absorbed. Repeat until all the water has been added (about 20 minutes). Add the soy sauce and season with white pepper.

Fold one end of a bamboo leaf on the diagonal to form a cone. Hold in one hand and spoon in 2 tablespoons of rice. Make an indent in the rice, add 1 tablespoon of eggplant filling, then top with 1 tablespoon of rice. Fold the other end of the leaf over to enclose the filling. Secure with a toothpick and tie tightly with string. Repeat with the remaining bamboo leaves, rice and filling. Place in a single layer inside a double bamboo steamer. Cover and put over a wok half filled with simmering water. Steam for 1½ hours, or until the rice is tender, adding more boiling water as needed. Serve hot.

Makes 20

Arancini

440 g (2 cups) risotto rice (arborio,
  vialone nano or carnaroli)
1 egg, lightly beaten
1 egg yolk
50 g (1/2 cup) grated Parmesan
  cheese
plain (all-purpose) flour
2 eggs, lightly beaten
dry breadcrumbs, to coat
oil, for deep-frying

Meat sauce
1 dried porcini mushroom
1 tablespoon olive oil
1 onion, chopped
125 g (4 1/2 oz) minced (ground) beef
  or veal
2 slices prosciutto, finely chopped
2 tablespoons tomato paste (purée)
80 ml (1/3 cup) white wine
1/2 teaspoon dried thyme leaves
3 tablespoons finely chopped parsley

Cook the rice in boiling water for
20 minutes, or until just soft. Drain,
without rinsing and cool. Put in a
large bowl and add the egg, egg
yolk and Parmesan. Stir until the rice
sticks together. Cover and set aside.

To make the meat sauce, soak the
porcini in hot water for 10 minutes,
then squeeze dry and chop finely.
Heat the oil in a frying pan. Add the
mushroom and onion and cook for
3 minutes, or until soft. Add the mince
and cook, stirring, until browned. Add
the prosciutto, tomato paste, wine,
thyme and pepper to taste. Cook,
stirring, for 5 minutes, or until all the
liquid is absorbed. Stir in the parsley
and set aside to cool. With wet
hands, form the rice mixture into
10 balls. Wet your hands again and
gently pull the balls apart. Place
3 teaspoons of the meat sauce in the
centre of each. Reshape to enclose
the filling. Roll in the flour, beaten egg
and breadcrumbs and chill for 1 hour.

Fill a deep heavy-based pan one-third
full of oil and heat to 180°C (350°F),
or until a cube of bread browns in
15 seconds. Deep-fry the croquettes,
two at a time, for 3–4 minutes, or until
golden. Drain on paper towels and
keep warm while cooking the rest.

Makes 10

Tamarind beef, bean and hokkien noodle stir-fry

Tamarind sauce
1 tablespoon tamarind purée
1 tablespoon vegetable oil
1 onion, finely diced
2 tablespoons palm sugar or soft
  brown sugar
2 tablespoons tamari

500 g (1 lb 2 oz) hokkien (egg)
  noodles (see Note, page 191)
4 beef fillet steaks (about 115 g/4 oz
  each)
2 tablespoons oil
3 garlic cloves, crushed
1 small chilli, seeded and diced
300 g (10½ oz) baby green beans,
  trimmed
100 g (3½ oz) sugar snap peas,
  trimmed
1 tablespoon mirin
15 g (¼ cup) finely chopped coriander
  (cilantro) leaves

To make the tamarind sauce, dilute the tamarind in 250 ml (1 cup) hot water. Heat the oil in a saucepan. Add the onion and cook over medium heat for 6–8 minutes, or until soft and golden. Add the palm sugar and stir until dissolved. Add the tamarind liquid and tamari and simmer for 5 minutes, or until thick.

Rinse the noodles in a colander with warm water to soften — separate with your hands. Drain.

Season the steaks with salt and freshly ground black pepper. Heat half the oil in a large frying pan. Add the steaks and cook on each side for 3–4 minutes, or until cooked to your liking. Remove from the pan and rest in a warm place.

Heat the remaining oil in a wok and cook the garlic and chilli over high heat for 30 seconds. Add the beans and peas and cook for 2 minutes. Stir in the mirin and coriander. Add the noodles and toss through to heat.

Divide the noodles among four plates. Top with the steak and drizzle with the tamarind sauce.

Serves 4

Chicken and pork paella

60 ml (¼ cup) olive oil
1 large red capsicum (pepper),
  seeded and cut into 5 mm (¼ inch)
  strips
600 g (1 lb 5 oz) chicken thigh fillets,
  cut into 3 cm (1¼ inch) cubes
200 g (7 oz) chorizo sausage, cut into
  2 cm (¾ inch) slices
200 g (7 oz) mushrooms, thinly sliced
3 garlic cloves, crushed
1 tablespoon lemon zest
700 g (1 lb 9 oz) tomatoes, roughly
  chopped
200 g (7 oz) green beans, cut into
  3 cm (1¼ inch) lengths
1 tablespoon chopped rosemary
2 tablespoons chopped flat-leaf
  (Italian) parsley
¼ teaspoon saffron threads dissolved
  in 60 ml (¼ cup) hot water
440 g (2 cups) short-grain rice
750 ml (3 cups) hot chicken stock
6 lemon wedges

Heat the oil in a large deep frying pan or paella pan over medium heat. Add the capsicum and cook for 6 minutes, or until soft. Remove from the pan.

Add the chicken to the pan and cook for 10 minutes, or until brown on all sides. Remove. Add the sausage to the pan and cook for 5 minutes, or until golden on all sides. Remove.

Add the mushrooms, garlic and lemon zest and cook over medium heat for 5 minutes. Stir in the tomato and capsicum and cook for a further 5 minutes, or until the tomato is soft.

Add the beans, rosemary, parsley, saffron mixture, rice, chicken and sausage. Stir briefly and then add the stock. Do not stir at this point. Reduce the heat and simmer for 30 minutes. Remove the pan from the heat, cover and leave to stand for 10 minutes. Serve with lemon wedges.

Serves 6

Note: Paellas are not stirred right to the bottom of the pan during cooking in the hope that a thin crust of crispy rice will form. This is considered one of the best parts of the paella. For this reason, do not use a non-stick frying pan. Paellas are traditionally served at the table from the pan.

Chiang mai noodles

250 g (9 oz) fresh thin egg noodles
2 tablespoons oil
6 red Asian shallots, finely chopped
3 garlic cloves, crushed
1–2 small red chillies, seeded and
  finely chopped
2–3 tablespoons red curry paste
375 g (13 oz) chicken breast fillet, cut
  into thin strips
2 tablespoons fish sauce
1 tablespoon grated palm sugar or
  soft brown sugar
750 ml (3 cups) coconut milk
1 tablespoon lime juice
250 ml (1 cup) chicken stock
4 spring onions (scallions), sliced,
  to garnish
10 g (⅓ cup) coriander (cilantro)
  leaves, to garnish
fried red Asian shallot flakes,
  to garnish
ready-made fried noodles, to garnish
red chilli, finely diced, to garnish

Cook the egg noodles in a saucepan of boiling water according to the packet instructions. Drain, cover and set aside.

Heat a large wok over high heat, add the oil and swirl to coat. Add the shallots, garlic and chilli and stir-fry for 3 minutes. Stir in the curry paste and stir-fry for 2 minutes. Add the chicken and stir-fry for 3 minutes, or until it changes colour.

Stir in the fish sauce, palm sugar, coconut milk, lime juice and stock. Reduce the heat and simmer over low heat for 5 minutes — do not boil.

To serve, divide the noodles among four deep serving bowls and spoon in the chicken mixture. Garnish with the spring onion, coriander, shallot flakes, fried noodles and chilli.

Serves 4

Phad Thai

250 g (9 oz) dried flat rice stick
  noodles
1 tablespoon tamarind purée
1 small red chilli, chopped
2 garlic cloves, chopped
2 spring onions (scallions), sliced
1½ tablespoons soft brown sugar
2 tablespoons fish sauce
2 tablespoons lime juice
2 tablespoons oil
2 eggs, beaten
150 g (5½ oz) pork fillet, thinly sliced
8 large raw prawns (shrimp), peeled
  and deveined, with tails intact
100 g (3½ oz) fried tofu puffs,
  julienned
90 g (1 cup) bean sprouts
40 g (¼ cup) chopped roasted
  peanuts
3 tablespoons coriander (cilantro)
  leaves
1 lime, cut into wedges

Place the noodles in a heatproof
bowl, cover with warm water and
soak for 15–20 minutes, or until the
noodles are *al dente*. Drain well.

Combine the tamarind purée with
1 tablespoon water. Place the chilli,
garlic and spring onion in a spice
grinder (or use a mortar and pestle)
and grind to a smooth paste. Transfer
the mixture to a bowl and stir in the
tamarind mixture along with the sugar,
fish sauce and lime juice, stirring until
the ingredients are combined.

Heat a wok until very hot, add
1 tablespoon of the oil and swirl to
coat the side. Add the egg, swirl to
coat and cook for 1–2 minutes, or
until set. Remove the egg, roll it up
and cut into thin slices.

Heat the remaining oil in the wok, stir
in the chilli mixture and stir-fry for
30 seconds. Add the pork and stir-fry
for 2 minutes, or until tender. Add the
prawns and stir-fry for a further
minute, or until pink and curled.

Stir in the noodles, egg, tofu puffs
and the bean sprouts and gently toss
together until heated through. Serve
immediately topped with the peanuts,
coriander and lime wedges.

Serves 4–6

Risotto Milanese

185 ml (¾ cup) dry white vermouth
or white wine
1 large pinch saffron strands
1.5 litres (6 cups) chicken stock
100 g (3½ oz) butter
70 g (2½ oz) beef marrow
1 large onion, finely chopped
1 garlic clove, crushed
350 g (12 oz) risotto rice (arborio,
vialone nano or carnaroli)
150 g (5½ oz) Parmesan cheese,
grated

Put the vermouth in a bowl, add the saffron and soak for 10 minutes. Heat the chicken stock in a saucepan and maintain at a low simmer.

Melt the butter and beef marrow in a deep heavy-based saucepan and gently cook the onion and garlic until softened but not browned. Add the rice and reduce the heat to low. Season, and stir to coat the grains of rice in the butter and marrow.

Add the vermouth and saffron to the rice and increase the heat to medium. Cook, stirring, until all the liquid has been absorbed.

Stir in a ladleful of the stock and cook at a fast simmer, stirring continuously. When the stock has been absorbed, stir in another ladleful. Continue like this for about 20 minutes, or until the rice is *al dente*. Add a little more stock or water if you need to — every risotto will use a different amount.

Stir in 100 g (3½ oz) of the Parmesan cheese and sprinkle the rest over the top to serve.

Serves 4

Note: This dish is the classic accompaniment to osso buco but is also perfect as a first course.

Soba noodles with miso and baby eggplant

250 g (9 oz) soba noodles
3 teaspoons dashi granules
1 1/2 tablespoons yellow miso paste
1 1/2 tablespoons Japanese soy sauce
1 1/2 tablespoons mirin
2 tablespoons vegetable oil
1/2 teaspoon sesame oil
6 baby eggplants (aubergines), cut
    into 1 cm (1/2 inch) slices
2 garlic cloves, crushed
1 tablespoon finely chopped ginger
150 g (1 cup) cooked peas
2 spring onions (scallions), sliced
    thinly on the diagonal
toasted sesame seeds, to garnish

Cook the noodles in a large saucepan of boiling water for 5 minutes. Drain and refresh with cold water.

Dissolve the dashi granules in 375 ml (1 1/2 cups) boiling water. Stir in the miso paste, soy sauce and mirin.

Heat half the oils in a large frying pan over high heat. Cook the eggplant in two batches, for 4 minutes, or until golden on both sides. (Use the remaining oil to cook the second batch of eggplant.)

Stir in the garlic and ginger, then the miso mixture and bring to the boil. Reduce the heat and simmer for 10 minutes, or until slightly thickened and the eggplant is cooked. Add the noodles and peas and cook for 2 minutes, or until heated through.

Serve the noodles in shallow bowls and garnish with spring onion and toasted sesame seeds.

Serves 4

Mongolian hotpot

250 g (9 oz) dried rice vermicelli
600 g (1 lb 5 oz) lamb backstraps,
  thinly sliced across the grain
4 spring onions (scallions), sliced
1.5 litres (6 cups) light chicken stock
3 x 6 cm (1 1/4 x 2 1/2 inch) piece ginger,
  cut into 6 slices
2 tablespoons Chinese rice wine
300 g (10 1/2 oz) silken firm tofu, cut
  into 1.5 cm (5/8 inch) cubes
300 g (10 1/2 oz) Chinese broccoli (gai
  larn), cut into 4 cm (1 1/2 inch)
  lengths
75 g (1 2/3 cups) shredded Chinese
  cabbage

Sauce
80 ml (1/3 cup) light soy sauce
2 tablespoons Chinese sesame paste
1 tablespoon Chinese rice wine
1 teaspoon chilli and garlic paste

Place the vermicelli in a large heatproof bowl, cover with boiling water and soak for 6–7 minutes. Drain well and divide among six serving bowls. Top with the lamb slices and spring onion.

To make the sauce, combine the soy sauce, sesame paste, rice wine and the chilli and garlic paste in a bowl.

Put the stock, ginger and rice wine in a 2.5 litre (10 cup) flameproof hotpot or large saucepan. Cover and bring to the boil over high heat. Add the tofu, Chinese broccoli and Chinese cabbage and simmer, uncovered, for 1 minute, or until the broccoli has wilted. Divide the tofu, broccoli and cabbage among the serving bowls, then ladle on the hot stock. Drizzle a little of the sauce on top and serve the rest on the side.

Serves 6

Notes: Make sure the stock is hot enough to cook the thin slices of lamb. This recipe traditionally uses a Chinese steamboat. This is an aluminium pot with a steam spout in the middle, which is placed on a propane burner in the middle of the dining table. You could use a fondue pot instead.

Sweet potato and sage risotto

8 slices prosciutto
1.25 litres (5 cups) chicken stock
100 ml (3½ fl oz) extra virgin olive oil
1 red onion, cut into thin wedges
600 g (1 lb 5 oz) orange sweet
   potato, peeled, cut into 2.5 cm
   (1 inch) cubes
440 g (2 cups) risotto rice (arborio,
   vialone nano or carnaroli)
75 g (¾ cup) shaved Parmesan
   cheese
3 tablespoons shredded sage
shaved Parmesan cheese, extra,
   to serve

Place the prosciutto slices under a hot grill (broiler) and grill (broil) for 1–2 minutes each side, or until crispy.

Heat the chicken stock in a saucepan, cover and keep at a low simmer.

Heat 60 ml (¼ cup) of the oil in a large saucepan, add the onion and cook over medium heat for 2–3 minutes, or until softened. Add the sweet potato and rice and stir through until well coated in the oil.

Stir in a ladleful of the hot stock and cook over moderate heat, stirring continuously. When the stock has been absorbed, stir in another ladleful. Continue like this for about 20 minutes, or until all the stock has been added and the rice is creamy and *al dente*. (You may not need to use all the stock, or you may need a little extra.)

Stir in the shaved Parmesan and 2 tablespoons of the sage. Season. Spoon into four bowls and drizzle with the remaining oil. Break the prosciutto into pieces and sprinkle over the top with the remaining sage. Top with the extra Parmesan, if desired, and serve.

Serves 4

Lamb with hokkien noodles and sour sauce

450 g (1 lb) hokkien (egg) noodles
(see Note)
2 tablespoons vegetable oil
375 g (13 oz) lamb backstrap, thinly
sliced against the grain
70 g (2½ oz) red Asian shallots,
peeled and thinly sliced
3 garlic cloves, crushed
2 teaspoons finely chopped ginger
1 small red chilli, seeded and finely
chopped
1½ tablespoons red curry paste
125 g (4½ oz) snow peas
(mangetout), trimmed and cut
in half on the diagonal
1 small carrot, julienned
125 ml (½ cup) chicken stock
15 g (½ oz) palm sugar, grated, or
soft brown sugar
1 tablespoon lime juice
small whole basil leaves, to garnish

Put the noodles in a bowl, cover with boiling water and soak for 1 minute. Drain and set aside.

Heat 1 tablespoon of the oil in a wok and swirl to coat the side. Stir-fry the lamb in batches over high heat for 2–3 minutes, or until it just changes colour. Remove to a side plate.

Add the remaining oil, then the shallots, garlic, ginger and chilli and stir-fry for 1–2 minutes. Stir in the curry paste and cook for 1 minute. Add the snow peas, carrot and the lamb and combine. Cook over high heat, tossing often, for 1–2 minutes.

Add the stock, palm sugar and lime juice, toss to combine and cook for 2–3 minutes. Add the noodles and cook for 1 minute, or until heated through. Divide among serving bowls and garnish with the basil.

Serves 4–6

Note: Hokkien noodles are thick, fresh egg noodles that have been cooked and lightly oiled before packaging. They are usually sold vacuum packed.

Sukiyaki

Sauce
1/2–1 teaspoon dashi granules
80 ml (1/3 cup) soy sauce
2 tablespoons sake
2 tablespoons mirin
1 tablespoon caster (superfine) sugar

300 g (10 1/2 oz) shirataki noodles (see Notes)
50 g (1 3/4 oz) lard
5 large spring onions (scallions), cut into 1 cm (1/2 inch) slices on the diagonal
16 fresh shiitake mushrooms (180 g/6 1/2 oz), cut into smaller pieces if too large
800 g (1 lb 12 oz) rump steak, thinly sliced across the grain (wrap the beef in plastic wrap and freeze for 40 minutes before cutting, as this will make it easier to slice)
100 g (3 1/2 oz) watercress, trimmed
4 eggs (optional)

To make the sauce, dissolve the dashi granules in 125 ml (1/2 cup) water in a bowl. Stir in the soy sauce, sake, mirin and caster sugar.

Drain the noodles, place in a large heatproof bowl, cover with boiling water and soak for 2 minutes. Rinse in cold water and drain well.

Melt the lard in a large frying pan over medium heat. Cook the spring onion, mushrooms and beef in batches, stirring continuously, for 1–2 minutes each batch, or until just brown. Return all the meat, spring onion and mushrooms to the pan, then add the sauce and watercress. Cook for 1 minute, or until the watercress has wilted — the sauce needs to just cover the ingredients.

To serve, divide the noodles among four serving bowls and spoon the sauce evenly over the top. If desired, crack an egg into each bowl and break up through the soup using chopsticks until it partially cooks.

Serves 4

Notes: Shirataki noodles are sold in the refrigerated section in Japanese supermarkets. You can also use dried rice vermicelli — soak in boiling water for 5 minutes before use.

Vegetarian paella

200 g (1 cup) dried haricot beans
1/4 teaspoon saffron threads
2 tablespoons olive oil
1 onion, diced
1 red capsicum (pepper), cut into
    1 x 4 cm (1/2 x 1 1/2 inch) strips
5 garlic cloves, crushed
275 g (1 1/4 cups) paella or arborio rice
1 tablespoon sweet paprika
1/2 teaspoon mixed spice
750 ml (3 cups) vegetable stock
400 g (14 oz) can chopped tomatoes
1 1/2 tablespoons tomato paste (purée)
150 g (5 1/2 oz) fresh or frozen soya
    beans (see Note)
100 g (3 1/2 oz) silverbeet (Swiss chard)
    leaves (no stems), shredded
400 g (14 oz) can artichoke hearts,
    drained and quartered
4 tablespoons chopped coriander
    (cilantro) leaves

Put the haricot beans in a bowl, cover with cold water and soak overnight. Drain and rinse well. Place the saffron threads in a small frying pan over medium–low heat. Dry-fry, shaking the pan, for 1 minute, or until darkened. Remove from the heat and, when cool, crumble into a small bowl. Pour in 125 ml (1/2 cup) warm water and allow to steep.

Heat the oil in a large paella or frying pan. Add the onion and capsicum and cook over medium–high heat for 4–5 minutes, or until the onion is soft. Stir in the garlic and cook for 1 minute. Reduce the heat and add the beans, rice, paprika, mixed spice and 1/2 teaspoon salt. Stir to coat. Add the saffron water, stock, tomato and tomato paste and bring to the boil. Cover, reduce the heat and simmer for 20 minutes.

Stir in the soya beans, silverbeet and artichoke hearts and cook, covered, for 8 minutes, or until all the liquid is absorbed and the rice and beans are tender. Turn off the heat and leave for 5 minutes. Stir in the coriander just before serving.

Serves 6

Note: Fresh or frozen soya beans are available from Asian grocery stores.

Fish hotpot with ginger and tomatoes

1 tablespoon peanut oil
1 onion, cut into thin wedges
1 small red chilli, sliced
3 garlic cloves, finely chopped
2 x 2 cm (³/₄ x ³/₄ inch) piece ginger, julienned
½ teaspoon ground turmeric
400 g (14 oz) can chopped tomatoes
1 litre (4 cups) chicken stock
1 tablespoon tamarind purée
85 g (3 oz) dried flat rice stick noodles
600 g (1 lb 5 oz) snapper fillets, skin removed, cut into 3 cm (1¼ inch) cubes
coriander (cilantro) leaves, to garnish

Preheat the oven to 220°C (425°F/ Gas 7). Heat the oil in a frying pan over medium–high heat and cook the onion for 1–2 minutes, or until soft. Add the chilli, garlic and ginger and cook for a further 30 seconds. Add the turmeric, tomato, chicken stock and tamarind purée and bring to the boil over high heat. Transfer to a 2.5 litre (10 cup) heatproof hotpot or casserole dish and cook, covered, in the oven for 40 minutes.

Place the noodles in a large heatproof bowl, cover with warm water and soak for 15–20 minutes, or until *al dente*. Drain, rinse and drain again.

Remove the hotpot from the oven and stir in the noodles. Add the fish cubes, then cover and return to the oven for a further 10 minutes, or until the fish is cooked through. Serve sprinkled with some coriander leaves.

Serves 4

Chicken and mushroom risotto

1.25 litres (5 cups) vegetable or
  chicken stock
2 tablespoons olive oil
300 g (10½ oz) chicken breast fillets,
  cut into 1.5 cm (⅝ inch) wide strips
250 g (9 oz) small button mushrooms,
  halved
pinch nutmeg
2 garlic cloves, crushed
20 g (¾ oz) butter
1 small onion, finely chopped
385 g (1¾ cups) risotto rice (arborio,
  vialone nano or carnaroli)
170 ml (⅔ cup) dry white wine
3 tablespoons sour cream
50 g (½ cup) grated Parmesan
  cheese
3 tablespoons finely chopped flat-leaf
  (Italian) parsley

Bring the stock to the boil over high heat, reduce the heat and keep at a low simmer.

Heat the oil in a large saucepan. Cook the chicken pieces over high heat for 3–4 minutes, or until golden brown. Add the mushrooms and cook for 1–2 minutes more, or until starting to brown. Stir in the nutmeg and garlic, season with salt and freshly ground black pepper and cook for 30 seconds. Remove from the pan.

Melt the butter in the same saucepan and cook the onion over low heat for 5–6 minutes. Add the rice, stir to coat, then stir in the wine. Once the wine is absorbed, stir in a ladleful of the hot stock and cook over moderate heat, stirring continuously. When the stock has been absorbed, stir in another ladleful. Continue like this for about 20 minutes, or until all the stock has been added and the rice is creamy and *al dente*. (You may not need to use all the stock, or you may need a little extra.) Stir in the mushrooms and the chicken with the last of the stock.

Remove the pan from the heat and stir in the sour cream, Parmesan and parsley. Season before serving.

Serves 4

Seafood noodles

6 dried shiitake mushrooms
400 g (14 oz) fresh thick egg noodles
1 egg white, lightly beaten
3 teaspoons cornflour (cornstarch)
1 teaspoon crushed Sichuan
  peppercorns
250 g (9 oz) firm white fish, cut into
  2 cm (3/4 inch) cubes
200 g (7 oz) raw prawns (shrimp),
  peeled and deveined, with tails intact
3 tablespoons peanut oil
3 spring onions (scallions), sliced on
  the diagonal
2 garlic cloves, crushed
1 tablespoon grated ginger
225 g (8 oz) can bamboo shoots,
  thinly sliced
2 tablespoons hot chilli sauce
1 tablespoon soy sauce
2 tablespoons rice wine
185 ml (3/4 cup) fish stock

Soak the mushrooms in 125 ml
(1/2 cup) warm water for 20 minutes.
Drain. Discard the stems, then thinly
slice the caps.

Cook the noodles in a saucepan of
boiling water for 2–3 minutes, or until
just tender. Drain.

Blend the egg white, cornflour and
half the peppercorns to a smooth
paste. Dip the seafood into the
mixture. Heat 2 tablespoons of the oil
in a wok. Drain the excess batter from
the seafood and stir-fry in batches
over high heat until crisp and golden.
Drain on paper towels.

Clean the wok and heat the remaining
oil. Toss the spring onion, garlic,
ginger, bamboo shoots, mushrooms,
and remaining pepper over high heat
for 1 minute. Stir in the chilli sauce,
soy sauce, rice wine, fish stock and
noodles. Add the seafood and toss
until heated through.

Serves 4

Pancit canton

1 1/2 tablespoons peanut oil
1 large onion, finely chopped
2 garlic cloves, finely chopped
2 x 2 cm (3/4 x 3/4 inch) piece ginger,
  shredded
500 g (1 lb 2 oz) chicken thigh fillets,
  trimmed and cut into 2 cm (3/4 inch)
  pieces
175 g (6 oz) Chinese cabbage,
  shredded
1 carrot, julienned
200 g (7 oz) Chinese barbecued pork
  (char sui), cut into 5 mm (1/4 inch)
  thick pieces
3 teaspoons Chinese rice wine
2 teaspoons sugar
150 g (5 1/2 oz) snow peas
  (mangetout), trimmed
375 ml (1 1/2 cups) chicken stock
1 tablespoon light soy sauce
225 g (8 oz) pancit canton (or Chinese
  e-fu) noodles (see Note)
1 lemon, cut into wedges

Heat a wok over high heat, add the oil and swirl to coat. Add the onion and cook for 2 minutes, then add the garlic and ginger and cook for 1 minute. Add the chicken and cook for 2–3 minutes, or until browned. Stir in the cabbage, carrot, pork, rice wine and sugar and cook for a further 3–4 minutes, or until the pork is heated and the vegetables are soft. Add the snow peas and cook for 1 minute. Remove the mixture from the wok.

Add the chicken stock and soy sauce to the wok and bring to the boil. Add the noodles and cook, stirring, for 3–4 minutes, or until soft and almost cooked through.

Return the stir-fry mixture to the wok and toss with the noodles for 1 minute, or until combined. Divide among four warmed serving dishes and garnish with lemon wedges.

Serves 4

Note: Pancit canton noodles are used mostly in the Philippines and China, where they are called 'birthday' or 'long-life' noodles — their length denotes a long life for those who eat them. These round cakes of pre-boiled, deep-fried noodles are delicate and break easily. They are available in Asian grocery stores.

Lion's head meatballs

6 dried Chinese mushrooms
100 g (3½ oz) cellophane noodles
  (mung bean vermicelli)
600 g (1 lb 5 oz) minced (ground)
  pork
1 egg white
4 garlic cloves, finely chopped
1 tablespoon finely grated ginger
1 tablespoon cornflour (cornstarch)
1½ tablespoons Chinese rice wine
6 spring onions (scallions), thinly
  sliced
500 ml (2 cups) good-quality chicken
  stock
2 tablespoons peanut oil
60 ml (¼ cup) light soy sauce
1 teaspoon sugar
400 g (14 oz) bok choy (pak choi), cut
  in half lengthways and leaves
  separated

Soak the mushrooms in 250 ml (1 cup) boiling water for 20 minutes. Drain. Discard the stems and thinly slice the caps. Put the noodles in a heatproof bowl, cover with boiling water and soak for 3–4 minutes, or until soft. Drain and rinse. Preheat the oven to 220°C (425°F/Gas 7).

Place the mince, egg white, garlic, ginger, cornflour, rice wine, two-thirds of the spring onion and a pinch of salt in a food processor. Using the pulse button, process until smooth and well combined. Divide the mixture into eight portions and, using wet hands, shape into large balls.

Put the stock in a large saucepan and bring to the boil over high heat, then remove from the heat and keep warm.

Heat the oil in a wok over high heat. Fry the meatballs in batches for 2 minutes each side, or until golden, but not cooked through. Drain. Place the meatballs, mushrooms, soy sauce and sugar in a 2.5 litre (10 cup) ovenproof clay pot or casserole dish and cover with the hot stock. Bake, covered, for 45 minutes. Add the bok choy and noodles and bake, covered, for 10 minutes. Sprinkle with the remaining spring onion and serve.

Serves 4

Idiyappam

225 g (8 oz) rice sticks or vermicelli
4 tablespoons oil
50 g (⅓ cup) cashew nuts
½ onion, chopped
3 eggs
150 g (1 cup) fresh or frozen peas
10 curry leaves
2 carrots, grated
2 leeks, finely shredded
1 red capsicum (pepper), diced
2 tablespoons tomato sauce
 (ketchup)
1 tablespoon soy sauce
1 teaspoon salt

Soak the rice sticks in cold water for 30 minutes, then drain and put them in a saucepan of boiling water. Remove from the heat and leave in the pan for 3 minutes. Drain and refresh in cold water.

Heat 1 tablespoon of the oil in a frying pan and fry the cashews until golden. Remove, add the onion to the pan, fry until dark golden, then drain on paper towels. Cook the eggs in boiling water for 10 minutes to hard-boil, then cool immediately in cold water. When cold, peel them and cut into wedges. Cook the peas in boiling water until tender.

Heat the remaining oil in a frying pan and briefly fry the curry leaves. Add the carrot, leek and capsicum and stir for 1 minute. Add the tomato sauce, soy sauce, salt and rice sticks and mix, stirring constantly to prevent the rice sticks from sticking to the pan. Serve on a platter and garnish with the peas, cashews, fried onion and egg wedges.

Serves 4

Tofu puffs with mushrooms and round rice noodles

8 dried shiitake mushrooms
500 g (1 lb 2 oz) fresh round rice
    noodles
3 litres (12 cups) good-quality chicken
    stock
1 carrot, thinly sliced on the diagonal
100 g (3½ oz) fried tofu puffs, cut
    in half
800 g (1 lb 12 oz) bok choy (pak
    choi), trimmed and quartered
1–1½ tablespoons mushroom soy
    sauce
6 drops sesame oil
ground white pepper, to season
100 g (3½ oz) enoki mushrooms,
    ends trimmed

Place the shiitake mushrooms in a heatproof bowl, cover with boiling water and soak for 20 minutes. Drain and remove the stems, squeezing out any excess water.

Meanwhile, place the noodles in a heatproof bowl, cover with boiling water and soak briefly. Gently separate the noodles with your hands and drain well.

Place the chicken stock in a large saucepan, cover and slowly heat over low heat.

Add the noodles to the simmering stock along with the carrot, tofu puffs, shiitake mushrooms and bok choy. Cook for 1–2 minutes, or until the carrot and noodles are tender and the bok choy has wilted slightly. Stir in the soy sauce and sesame oil and season to taste with white pepper.

Divide the noodles, vegetables, tofu puffs and enoki mushrooms among four serving bowls, ladle the broth on top and serve immediately.

Serves 4

Roast pork, Chinese cabbage and noodle hotpot

70 g (2½ oz) cellophane noodles
  (mung bean vermicelli)
250 g (9 oz) Chinese cabbage
1 litre (4 cups) chicken stock
2.5 x 2.5 cm (1 x 1 inch) piece ginger,
  thinly sliced
350 g (12 oz) Chinese roast pork, skin
  removed and reserved (see Note)
2 spring onions (scallions), thinly
  sliced on the diagonal
2 tablespoons light soy sauce
1 tablespoon Chinese rice wine
½ teaspoon sesame oil

Soak the noodles in boiling water for 3–4 minutes. Drain and rinse, then drain again.

Separate the cabbage leaves and cut the leafy ends from the stems. Cut both the cabbage stems and leaves into 2–3 cm (³/₄–1¼ inch) squares.

Place the stock and ginger slices in a 2 litre (8 cup) flameproof casserole dish and bring to the boil over high heat. Add the cabbage stems and cook for 2 minutes, then add the cabbage leaves and cook for 1 minute. Reduce the heat to medium, add the noodles and cook, covered, for 4–5 minutes, stirring occasionally.

Meanwhile, cut the pork into 2 cm (³/₄ inch) cubes and add the spring onion, soy sauce, rice wine and sesame oil. Stir to combine, then cook, covered, for 3–4 minutes and then serve.

Serves 4

Note: If desired, grill (broil) the reserved pork skin for 1 minute, or until crispy, and arrange on top of each serving.

Porcini risotto

30 g (1 oz) dried porcini mushrooms
1 litre (4 cups) chicken or vegetable
  stock
100 g (3½ oz) butter
1 onion, finely chopped
250 g (9 oz) mushrooms, sliced
2 garlic cloves, crushed
385 g (1¾ cups) risotto rice (arborio,
  vialone nano or carnaroli)
pinch of ground nutmeg
1 tablespoon finely chopped parsley
45 g (1½ oz) Parmesan cheese,
  grated

Put the porcini in a bowl, cover with 500 ml (2 cups) hot water and leave to soak for 15 minutes. Squeeze them dry, reserving the soaking liquid. If the porcini are large, roughly chop them. Strain the soaking liquid into a saucepan and add enough stock to make up to 1 litre (4 cups). Heat up and maintain at a low simmer.

Melt the butter in a deep heavy-based frying pan and gently cook the onion until soft but not browned. Add the mushrooms and porcini and fry for a few minutes. Add the garlic, stir briefly, then add the rice and reduce the heat to low. Season and stir to coat the grains of rice in the butter.

Increase the heat to medium and add a ladleful of the stock. Cook at a fast simmer, stirring constantly. When the stock has been absorbed, stir in another ladleful. Continue like this for about 20 minutes, or until the rice is creamy and *al dente*. Add a little more stock or water if you need to — every risotto will use a different amount.

Stir in the nutmeg, parsley and half the Parmesan, then serve with the rest of the Parmesan sprinkled over the top.

Serves 4

Lamb hotpot with rice noodles

2 garlic cloves, crushed
2 teaspoons grated ginger
1 teaspoon five-spice powder
1/4 teaspoon ground white pepper
2 tablespoons Chinese rice wine
1 teaspoon sugar
1 kg (2 lb 4 oz) boneless lamb
  shoulder, trimmed and cut into 3 cm
  (1 1/4 inch) pieces
30 g (1 oz) whole dried Chinese
  mushrooms
1 tablespoon peanut oil
1 large onion, cut into wedges
2 cm (3/4 inch) piece ginger, julienned
1 teaspoon Sichuan peppercorns,
  crushed or ground
2 tablespoons sweet bean paste
1 teaspoon black peppercorns,
  ground and toasted
500 ml (2 cups) chicken stock
60 ml (1/4 cup) oyster sauce
2 star anise
60 ml (1/4 cup) Chinese rice wine, extra
80 g (2 3/4 oz) can sliced bamboo
  shoots, drained
100 g (3 1/2 oz) can water chestnuts,
  drained and sliced
400 g (14 oz) fresh rice noodles, cut
  into 2 cm (3/4 inch) wide strips
1 spring onion (scallion), sliced on the
  diagonal

Combine the garlic, grated ginger, five-spice powder, white pepper, rice wine, sugar and 1 teaspoon salt in a large bowl. Add the lamb and toss to coat. Cover and marinate for 2 hours.

Meanwhile, soak the mushrooms in boiling water for 20 minutes. Drain. Discard the stems and slice the caps.

Heat a wok over high heat, add the oil and swirl to coat. Stir-fry the onion, julienned ginger and Sichuan pepper for 2 minutes. Cook the lamb in three batches, stir-frying for 2–3 minutes each batch, or until starting to brown. Stir in the bean paste and ground peppercorns and cook for 3 minutes, or until the lamb is brown. Add the stock and transfer to a 2 litre (8 cup) flameproof clay pot or casserole dish. Stir in the oyster sauce, star anise and extra rice wine and simmer, covered, over low heat for 1 1/2 hours, or until the lamb is tender. Stir in the bamboo shoots and water chestnuts and cook for 20 minutes. Add the mushrooms.

Cover the noodles with boiling water and gently separate. Drain and rinse, then add to the hotpot, stirring for 1–2 minutes, or until heated through. Sprinkle with the spring onion.

Serves 4

Shabu shabu

300 g (10½ oz) beef fillet, trimmed
1.5 litres (6 cups) chicken stock
2 x 6 cm (¾ x 2½ inch) piece ginger,
  thinly sliced
80 ml (⅓ cup) light soy sauce
2 tablespoons mirin
1 teaspoon sesame oil
200 g (7 oz) fresh udon noodles
150 g (5½ oz) English spinach, stems
  removed and thinly sliced
400 g (14 oz) Chinese cabbage
  (leaves only), finely shredded
100 g (3½ oz) fresh shiitake
  mushrooms, stems removed and
  caps thinly sliced
200 g (7 oz) firm tofu, cut into 2 cm
  (¾ inch) cubes
80 ml (⅓ cup) ready-made ponzu
  sauce or 60 ml (¼ cup) soy sauce
  combined with 1 tablespoon lemon
  juice

Wrap the beef fillet in plastic wrap and freeze for 40 minutes, or until it begins to harden. Remove and slice as thinly as possible across the grain.

Place the stock, ginger, soy sauce, mirin and sesame oil in a 2.5 litre (10 cup) flameproof casserole dish or hotpot over medium heat and simmer for 3 minutes. Add the noodles, gently stir with chopsticks to separate them, and cook for 1–2 minutes. Add the spinach, cabbage, mushrooms and tofu and simmer for 1 minute, or until the leaves have wilted.

Divide the noodles among four serving bowls using tongs, and top with the beef slices, vegetables and tofu. Ladle the hot stock on top and serve the ponzu sauce on the side.

Serves 4

Note: Traditionally, raw beef slices are arranged on a plate with the tofu, mushrooms, vegetables and noodles. The stock and seasoning are heated on a portable gas flame at the table. Guests dip the meat and vegetables in the hot stock and eat as they go, dipping into the dipping sauce. The noodles are added at the end and served with the broth.

Indonesian-style fried noodles

400 g (14 oz) fresh flat egg noodles
(5 mm/¼ inch wide)
2 tablespoons peanut oil
4 red Asian shallots, thinly sliced
2 garlic cloves, chopped
1 small red chilli, finely diced
200 g (7 oz) pork fillet, thinly sliced
across the grain
200 g (7 oz) chicken breast fillet, thinly
sliced
200 g (7 oz) small raw prawns
(shrimp), peeled and deveined, with
tails intact
2 Chinese cabbage leaves, shredded
2 carrots, cut in half lengthways and
thinly sliced
100 g (3½ oz) snake beans, cut into
3 cm (1¼ inch) lengths
60 ml (¼ cup) kecap manis
1 tablespoon light soy sauce
2 tomatoes, peeled, seeded and
chopped
4 spring onions (scallions), sliced on
the diagonal
1 tablespoon crisp fried onion flakes
flat-leaf (Italian) parsley, to garnish

Cook the noodles in a large saucepan of boiling water for 1 minute, or until tender. Drain and rinse them under cold water.

Heat a wok over high heat, add the oil and swirl to coat. Stir-fry the Asian shallots for 30 seconds. Add the garlic, chilli and pork and stir-fry for 2 minutes, then add the chicken and cook a further 2 minutes, or until the meat is golden and tender.

Add the prawns and stir-fry for another 2 minutes, or until pink and just cooked. Stir in the cabbage, carrot and beans and cook for 3 minutes, then add the noodles and gently stir-fry for 4 minutes, or until heated through — taking care not to break up the noodles. Stir in the kecap manis, soy sauce, chopped tomato and spring onion and stir-fry for 1–2 minutes.

Season with salt and freshly ground black pepper. Garnish with the fried onion flakes and parsley.

Serves 4

Note: This dish, called *bahmi goreng* in Indonesian, is traditionally eaten with chopped roasted peanuts and sambal oelek on the side. It is also delicious with satay sauce.

Pulao with onions and spices

200 g (1 cup) basmati rice
500 ml (2 cups) chicken stock
6 tablespoons ghee or oil
5 cardamom pods
5 cm (2 inch) piece of cinnamon stick
6 cloves
8 black peppercorns
4 Indian bay leaves (cassia leaves)
1 onion, finely sliced

Wash the rice in a sieve under cold running water until the water from the rice runs clear. Drain.

Heat the stock to near boiling point in a saucepan.

Meanwhile, heat 2 tablespoons of the ghee over medium heat in a large heavy-based saucepan. Add the cardamom, cinnamon, cloves, peppercorns and bay leaves and fry for 1 minute. Reduce the heat to low, add the rice and stir constantly for 1 minute. Add the heated stock and some salt to the rice and bring rapidly to a boil. Cover and simmer over low heat for 15 minutes. Allow the rice to rest for 10 minutes before uncovering. Lightly fluff up the rice before serving.

Meanwhile, heat the remaining ghee in a frying pan over low heat and fry the onion until soft. Increase the heat and fry until the onion is dark brown. Drain on paper towels, then use as a garnish. Serve with casseroles or Indian curries.

Serves 4

Chicken with ponzu sauce and somen noodles

Ponzu sauce
1 tablespoon lemon juice
1 tablespoon lime juice
1 tablespoon rice vinegar
1 tablespoon tamari
1½ tablespoons mirin
2½ tablespoons Japanese soy sauce
5 cm (2 inch) piece kombu (kelp), wiped with a damp cloth
1 tablespoon bonito flakes

900 g (2 lb) chicken thighs, trimmed and cut in half across the bone
10 cm (4 inch) piece kombu (kelp)
200 g (7 oz) dried somen noodles
250 g (9 oz) shiitake mushrooms (cut into smaller pieces if too large)
1 carrot, thinly sliced
300 g (10½ oz) baby English spinach leaves

To make the sauce, combine all the ingredients in a non-metallic bowl. Cover with plastic wrap and refrigerate overnight, then strain through a fine sieve.

Put the chicken and kombu in a pan with 875 ml (3½ cups) water. Bring to a simmer over medium heat and cook for 20 minutes, or until the chicken is cooked, skimming the scum off the surface. Remove the chicken and strain the broth. Transfer the broth and chicken pieces to a 2.5 litre (10 cup) flameproof casserole dish or Japanese nabe. Cover and continue to cook over low heat for 15 minutes.

Meanwhile, cook the noodles in a large saucepan of boiling water for 2 minutes, or until tender. Drain and rinse under cold running water.

Add the mushrooms and carrot to the chicken and cook for 5 minutes. Put the noodles on top of the chicken, then top with the spinach. Cover and cook for 2 minutes, or until the spinach has just wilted. Stir in 4–6 tablespoons of the ponzu sauce and serve.

Serves 4

Note: Traditionally, this dish would be served in a ceramic nabe dish, for the guests to help themselves.

Mee grob

4 Chinese dried mushrooms
oil, for deep-frying
100 g (3½ oz) dried rice vermicelli
100 g (3½ oz) fried tofu, cut into
  matchsticks
4 garlic cloves, crushed
1 onion, chopped
1 chicken breast fillet, thinly sliced
8 green beans, sliced on the diagonal
6 spring onions (scallions), thinly
  sliced on the diagonal
8 raw prawns (shrimp), peeled and
  deveined, with tails intact
30 g (⅓ cup) bean sprouts
coriander (cilantro) leaves, to garnish

Sauce
1 tablespoon soy sauce
3 tablespoons white vinegar
5 tablespoons sugar
3 tablespoons fish sauce
1 tablespoon sweet chilli sauce

Soak the mushrooms in boiling water
for 20 minutes. Drain, discard the
stems and thinly slice.

Fill a wok one-third full of oil and heat
to 180°C (350°F), or until a cube of
bread browns in 15 seconds. Cook
the vermicelli in small batches for
5 seconds, or until puffed and crispy.
Drain. Add the tofu to the wok in
batches and deep-fry for 1 minute, or
until crisp. Drain. Carefully remove all
but 2 tablespoons of oil.

Reheat the wok until very hot and
add the garlic and onion and stir-fry
for 1 minute. Add the chicken pieces,
mushrooms, beans and half the
spring onion. Stir-fry for 2 minutes, or
until the chicken has almost cooked
through. Add the prawns and stir-fry
for a further 2 minutes, or until they
just turn pink.

Combine all the sauce ingredients and
add to the wok. Stir-fry for 2 minutes,
or until the meat and prawns are
tender and the sauce is syrupy.

Remove from the heat and stir in the
vermicelli, tofu and bean sprouts.
Garnish with the coriander and
remaining sliced spring onion.

Serves 4–6

Steamed prawn rice noodle rolls

Dipping sauce
2 tablespoons light soy sauce
3 tablespoons rice vinegar

3 dried shiitake mushrooms
350 g (12 oz) raw prawns (shrimp), peeled and deveined
4 spring onions (scallions), chopped
60 g (2¼ oz) snow peas (mangetout), chopped
2 teaspoons finely chopped ginger
2 garlic cloves, crushed
15 g (½ cup) chopped coriander (cilantro) leaves
100 g (3½ oz) water chestnuts, chopped
1 teaspoon sesame oil
1 tablespoon light soy sauce
1 egg white
1 teaspoon cornflour (cornstarch)
300 g (10½ oz) fresh rice sheet noodles

To make the dipping sauce, combine the soy sauce and rice vinegar.

Cover the mushrooms with hot water and soak for 15 minutes. Drain, discard the stems and finely chop the caps.

Mince the prawns in a food processor. Add the mushrooms, spring onion, snow peas, ginger, garlic, coriander, water chestnuts, sesame oil, soy sauce and a pinch of salt. Add the egg white and cornflour and pulse until smooth.

Line a large bamboo steamer with baking paper and place over a wok of simmering water (ensure the base doesn't touch the water). Gently unfold the rice sheet noodle and cut into six 15 cm (6 inch) squares. Divide the filling between the six rice noodle squares and spread it out evenly over each. Roll firmly to form a log. Steam, covered, in a wok for 5 minutes. Cut each roll in half and serve with the sauce.

Makes 12

Risi e bisi

20 g (³/₄ oz) dried porcini mushrooms
1 litre (4 cups) vegetable or chicken
  stock
2 tablespoons olive oil
1 tablespoon butter
1 small onion, finely chopped
2 garlic cloves, crushed
385 g (1³/₄ cups) risotto rice (arborio,
  vialone nano or carnaroli)
250 g (9 oz) mushrooms, sliced
pinch of ground nutmeg
40 g (1¹/₂ oz) Parmesan cheese,
  grated
3 tablespoons finely chopped parsley

Soak the porcini in 500 ml (2 cups)
boiling water for 30 minutes. Drain,
reserving the liquid. Chop the porcini
and pass the liquid through a fine
sieve. Put the vegetable or chicken
stock in a saucepan, bring to the boil
and then maintain at a low simmer.

Heat the oil and butter in a large wide
heavy-based saucepan. Cook the
onion and garlic until softened but
not browned. Add the rice and reduce
the heat to low. Season and stir
briefly to thoroughly coat the rice.
Toss in the fresh mushrooms and
nutmeg. Season and cook, stirring,
for 1–2 minutes. Add the porcini and
the reserved soaking liquid, increase
the heat and cook until the liquid has
been absorbed.

Stir in a ladleful of hot stock and
cook over moderate heat, stirring
continuously. When the stock has
been absorbed, stir in another
ladleful. Continue like this for about
20 minutes, until all the stock has
been added and the rice is creamy
and al dente. (You may not need to
use all the stock, or you may need a
little extra.) Remove the pan from the
heat and stir in the Parmesan and
parsley. Season and serve.

Serves 4

Teriyaki beef with greens and crispy noodles

450 g (1 lb) sirloin steak, cut into thin
  strips
125 ml (½ cup) teriyaki marinade
vegetable oil, for deep-frying
100 g (3½ oz) dried rice vermicelli
2 tablespoons peanut oil
1 onion, sliced
3 garlic cloves, crushed
1 red chilli, seeded and finely
  chopped
200 g (7 oz) carrots, julienned
600 g (1 lb 5 oz) choy sum, cut into
  3 cm (1¼ inch) lengths
1 tablespoon lime juice

Combine the beef and teriyaki
marinade in a non-metallic bowl and
marinate for 2 hours.

Fill a wok one-third full of oil and heat
to 190°C (375°F), or until a cube of
bread browns in 10 seconds. Separate
the vermicelli noodles into small
bundles and deep-fry until they sizzle
and puff up. Drain well on paper
towels. Drain the oil and carefully
pour it into a heatproof bowl to cool
before discarding.

Heat 1 tablespoon of the peanut oil
in the wok. When the oil is nearly
smoking, add the beef (reserving the
marinade) and cook in batches over
high heat for 1–2 minutes. Remove to
a plate. Heat the remaining oil. Add
the onion and stir-fry for 3–4 minutes.
Add the garlic and chilli and cook for
30 seconds. Add the carrot and choy
sum and stir-fry for 3–4 minutes, or
until tender.

Return the beef to the wok with the
lime juice and reserved marinade and
cook over high heat for 3 minutes.
Add the noodles, toss well briefly, and
serve immediately.

Serves 4

Asparagus risotto

1 kg (2 lb 4 oz) asparagus
500 ml (2 cups) chicken stock
500 ml (2 cups) vegetable stock
4 tablespoons olive oil
1 small onion, finely chopped
360 g (1²/₃ cups) risotto rice (arborio, vialone nano or carnaroli)
70 g (2½ oz) Parmesan cheese, grated
3 tablespoons thick (double/heavy) cream

Wash the asparagus and remove the woody ends (hold each spear at both ends and bend it gently — it will snap at its natural breaking point). Separate the tender spear tips from the stems.

Cook the asparagus stems in boiling water for 8 minutes, or until very tender. Drain and place in a blender with the chicken and vegetable stocks. Blend for 1 minute, then put in a saucepan, bring to the boil and maintain at a low simmer.

Cook the asparagus tips in boiling water for 1 minute, drain and refresh in iced water.

Heat the oil in a large wide heavy-based saucepan. Add the onion and cook until soft but not browned. Stir in the rice, season, and reduce the heat to low. Stir in a ladleful of the stock and cook over moderate heat, stirring continuously. When the stock has been absorbed, stir in another ladleful. Continue like this for about 20 minutes, until all the stock has been added and the rice is *al dente*. (You may not use all the stock, or you may need a little extra — every risotto will be slightly different.) Add the Parmesan and cream and gently stir in the asparagus tips. Season.

Serves 4

Ma po tofu with noodles

450 g (1 lb) silken firm tofu, cut into
2 cm (³/₄ inch) cubes
375 g (13 oz) hokkien (egg) noodles
(see Note, page 191)
2 teaspoons cornflour (cornstarch)
1 tablespoon peanut oil
2 teaspoons finely chopped ginger
2 spring onions (scallions), finely
sliced on the diagonal
225 g (8 oz) minced (ground) pork
1¹/₂ tablespoons salted black beans,
rinsed and roughly chopped (see
Note)
1 tablespoon chilli bean paste
1 tablespoon dark soy sauce
125 ml (¹/₂ cup) chicken stock
1 tablespoon Chinese rice wine
2 garlic cloves, finely chopped
ground white pepper, to taste
2 spring onions (scallions), green part
only, extra, finely sliced on the
diagonal
¹/₂ teaspoon sesame oil

Place the tofu on paper towels to
drain the excess moisture.

Place the noodles in a heatproof
bowl, cover with boiling water and
soak for 1 minute, or until tender and
separated. Drain well, rinse under
cold water and drain again. Divide
among four serving bowls. Combine
the cornflour and 1 tablespoon water
in a small bowl.

Heat the oil in a wok over high heat.
Add the ginger and spring onion and
cook for 30 seconds, then add the
mince and stir-fry for 2 minutes, or
until almost cooked. Add the black
beans, chilli bean paste and soy
sauce and stir-fry for 1 minute. Stir in
the chicken stock, rice wine and tofu
and heat through.

Stir the cornflour mixture and garlic
into the wok and cook for a further
minute, or until thickened. Spoon over
the noodles and season with ground
white pepper. Garnish with the extra
spring onion and drizzle with the
sesame oil.

Serves 4

Note: Black beans are fermented and
heavily salted black soy beans. Rinse
before use. Available in cans and
packets from most Asian food stores.

Eggplant with buckwheat noodles

10 g (¼ oz) dried shiitake mushrooms
350 g (12 oz) buckwheat (soba)
  noodles
2 teaspoons sesame oil
3 tablespoons tahini
1 tablespoon light soy sauce
1 tablespoon dark soy sauce
1 tablespoon honey
2 tablespoons lemon juice
3 tablespoons peanut oil
2 long, thin eggplants (aubergines),
  cut into very thin strips
2 carrots, julienned
10 spring onions (scallions), cut on
  the diagonal
6 fresh shiitake mushrooms, thinly
  sliced
50 g (1 cup) roughly chopped
  coriander (cilantro) leaves

Soak the dried shiitake mushrooms in 125 ml (½ cup) hot water for 10 minutes. Drain, reserving the liquid. Discard the woody stems and finely slice the caps.

Cook the noodles in a saucepan of boiling water for 5 minutes, or until tender. Drain. Refresh under cold water, then toss with 1 teaspoon of the sesame oil.

Combine the tahini, light and dark soy sauces, honey, lemon juice, 2 tablespoons of the reserved mushroom liquid and the remaining teaspoon of sesame oil in a food processor until smooth.

Heat 2 tablespoons of the peanut oil over high heat. Add the eggplant and cook, turning often, for 4–5 minutes, or until soft and golden. Drain on paper towels.

Heat the remaining oil. Add the carrot, spring onion and fresh and dried mushrooms. Cook, stirring constantly, for 1–2 minutes, or until just softened. Remove from the heat and toss with the noodles, eggplant and dressing. Garnish with the coriander.

Serves 4–6

Hearty

Shepherd's pie

60 ml (1/4 cup) olive oil
1 large onion, finely chopped
2 garlic cloves, crushed
2 celery stalks, finely chopped
3 carrots, diced
2 bay leaves
1 tablespoon thyme, chopped
1 kg (2 lb 4 oz) good-quality minced
  (ground) lamb
1 1/2 tablespoons plain (all-purpose)
  flour
125 ml (1/2 cup) dry red wine
2 tablespoons tomato paste (purée)
400 g (14 oz) can crushed tomatoes
1.5 kg (3 lb 5 oz) floury potatoes
  (such as desiree), cut into even-size
  pieces
60 ml (1/4 cup) milk
100 g (3 1/2 oz) butter
1/2 teaspoon ground nutmeg

Heat 2 tablespoons of the oil over medium heat in a large heavy-based saucepan and cook the onion for 3–4 minutes, or until softened. Add the garlic, celery, carrot, bay leaves and thyme and cook for 2–3 minutes. Transfer to a bowl and remove the bay leaves.

Add the remaining oil to the same pan, add the mince and cook over high heat for 5–6 minutes, or until it changes colour. Mix in the flour, cook for 1 minute, then pour in the red wine and cook for 2–3 minutes. Return the vegetables to the pan with the tomato paste and crushed tomato. Reduce the heat, cover, and simmer for 45 minutes, stirring occasionally. Season, to taste, then transfer to a shallow 3 litre (12 cup) ovenproof dish and leave to cool. Preheat the oven to 180°C (350°F/Gas 4).

Meanwhile, boil the potatoes in salted water over medium heat for 20–25 minutes, or until tender. Drain, then mash with the milk and butter until smooth. Season with nutmeg and black pepper. Spoon over the mince and fluff with a fork. Bake for 30 minutes, or until golden and crusty.

Serves 6

Sausage and lentil stew

3 tablespoons olive oil
850 g (1 lb 14 oz) Italian sausages
1 onion, chopped
3 garlic cloves, thinly sliced
1 1/2 tablespoons chopped rosemary
2 x 400 g (14 oz) cans chopped
  tomatoes
16 juniper berries, lightly crushed
pinch of grated nutmeg
1 bay leaf
1 dried chilli, crushed
185 ml (3/4 cup) red wine
100 g (1/2 cup) green lentils

Heat the oil in a large saucepan and cook the sausages for 5–10 minutes, until browned. Remove the sausages from the pan and reduce the heat. Add the onion and garlic to the pan and cook gently until the onion is soft.

Stir in the rosemary and then add the tomato and cook gently until reduced to a thick sauce. Add the juniper berries, nutmeg, bay leaf, chilli, wine and 420 ml (1 2/3 cups) water. Bring to the boil, then add the lentils and sausages. Give the stew a good stir, cover the pan and simmer gently for about 40 minutes, or until the lentils are soft. Stir a couple of times to prevent the lentils sticking to the base of the pan. Add a little more water if the lentils are still not cooked.

Serves 4

Cornish pasties

310 g (2½ cups) plain (all-purpose)
    flour
125 g (4½ oz) butter, chilled and
    chopped
150 g (5½ oz) round steak, finely
    chopped
1 small potato, finely chopped
1 small onion, finely chopped
1 small carrot, finely chopped
1–2 teaspoons Worcestershire sauce
2 tablespoons beef stock
1 egg, lightly beaten

Grease a baking tray. Place the flour, butter and a pinch of salt in a food processor and process for 15 seconds, or until crumbly. Add 4–5 tablespoons of water and process in short bursts until the mixture comes together (add more water if needed). Turn out onto a floured surface and form into a ball. Cover with plastic wrap and chill for 30 minutes. Preheat the oven to 210°C (415°F/Gas 6–7).

Mix together the steak, potato, onion, carrot, Worcestershire sauce and stock. Season well.

Divide the dough into six portions and roll out each to 3 mm (⅛ inch) thick. Using a 16 cm (6½ inch) diameter plate as a guide, cut out six circles. Divide the filling evenly and put in the centre of each pastry circle.

Brush the edges of each pastry round with beaten egg and form into a semi-circle. Pinch the edges to form a frill and place on the tray. Brush with the remaining beaten egg and bake for 10 minutes. Lower the heat to 180°C (350°F/Gas 4). Cook for 20–25 minutes, or until golden.

Makes 6

Vegetable bake

4 large unpeeled potatoes, halved
600 g (1lb 5 oz) unpeeled orange
  sweet potatoes, halved
20 g (³/₄ oz) butter
1 tablespoon olive oil
2 large leeks, thinly sliced
3 garlic cloves, crushed
6 zucchini (courgettes), thinly sliced
  on the diagonal
300 ml (10½ fl oz) cream
130 g (1 cup) grated Parmesan
  cheese
1 tablespoon finely chopped thyme
1 tablespoon chopped flat-leaf (Italian)
  parsley
130 g (1 cup) grated Cheddar cheese

Preheat the oven to 180°C (350°F/
Gas 4) and grease a deep 2.5 litre
(10 cup) ovenproof dish. Boil the potato
and sweet potato for 10 minutes.

Meanwhile, heat the butter and oil in a
frying pan. Add the leek and cook
over low heat for 4–5 minutes, or until
softened. Add 1 garlic clove and the
zucchini and cook for 3–4 minutes, or
until the zucchini starts to soften.
Combine the cream, Parmesan, herbs
and remaining garlic and season.

When the potatoes and sweet potatoes
are cool, peel off the skins and thinly
slice. Layer half the potato slices in
the base of the dish. Season. Spread
with a quarter of the cream mixture,
then cover with the zucchini mixture,
patting down well. Top with another
quarter of the cream mixture. Use all
the sweet potato slices to make
another layer, and cover with half of
the remaining cream mixture. Top with
the remaining potato slices, then the
last of the cream mixture. Season and
top with the Cheddar.

Bake for 1¼ hours, or until the
vegetables are cooked. Cover with a
tented sheet of foil towards the end if
the top starts over-browning. Stand
for 10 minutes before cutting.

Serves 6

Baked beef vermicelli cake

85 g (3 oz) butter
1 onion, chopped
500 g (1 lb 2 oz) minced (ground) beef
800 g (1 lb 12 oz) bottled tomato
  pasta sauce
2 tablespoons tomato paste (purée)
250 g (9 oz) vermicelli or spaghettini
30 g (¼ cup) plain (all-purpose) flour
375 ml (1¼ cups) milk
155 g (1¼ cups) grated Cheddar
  cheese

Preheat the oven to 180°C (350°F/ Gas 4). Grease a 24 cm (9 inch) round deep springform tin. Melt 20 g (¾ oz) of the butter in a large deep frying pan and cook the onion over medium heat for 2–3 minutes, or until soft. Add the mince, breaking up any lumps with the back of a spoon, and cook for 4–5 minutes, or until browned. Stir in the pasta sauce and tomato paste, reduce the heat and simmer for 20–25 minutes. Season.

Cook the pasta in a large saucepan of boiling salted water until *al dente*. Drain and rinse. Meanwhile, melt the remaining butter in a saucepan over low heat. Stir in the flour and cook for 1 minute, or until pale and foaming. Remove from the heat and gradually stir in the milk. Return to the heat and stir constantly until the sauce boils and thickens. Reduce the heat and simmer for 2 minutes.

Spread half the pasta over the base of the tin, then cover with half the meat sauce. Cover with the remaining pasta, pressing it down. Spoon on the remaining meat sauce and then pour on the white sauce. Sprinkle with cheese and cook for 15 minutes. Stand for 10 minutes before removing from the tin. Cut into wedges.

Serves 4–6

Veal Parmigiana

60 ml (¼ cup) olive oil
1 garlic clove, crushed
pinch cayenne pepper
pinch caster (superfine) sugar
400 g (14 oz) can crushed tomatoes
3 teaspoons chopped oregano
40 g (⅓ cup) plain (all-purpose) flour
2 eggs
65 g (⅔ cup) dry breadcrumbs
4 large veal cutlets, well trimmed
100 g (3½ oz) mozzarella cheese,
thinly sliced
35 g (⅓ cup) grated Parmesan
cheese

Preheat the oven to 190°C (375°F/ Gas 5). Heat 1 tablespoon of the oil in a small pan over medium heat, add the garlic and cook for 30 seconds. Add the cayenne, sugar, tomato and half the oregano and cook, stirring occasionally, for 20 minutes, or until thickened. Season well. Place the flour in a wide shallow bowl and season well. Beat the eggs with 2 tablespoons of water in another bowl. Mix the breadcrumbs with the remaining oregano, season and place in a third bowl.

Pound the cutlets between two sheets of plastic wrap until flattened to 5 mm (¼ inch) thick, taking care not to tear the flesh from the bone. Coat in the seasoned flour, shaking off the excess, then dip both sides in the egg mixture and then coat in the breadcrumbs. Heat the remaining oil in a large frying pan. Add the cutlets in two batches and brown over medium–high heat for 2 minutes on each side. Transfer to a shallow baking dish large enough to fit them side by side.

Spread the sauce over each cutlet. Cover with the mozzarella and sprinkle with the Parmesan. Bake for 20 minutes, or until the cheeses have melted and browned. Serve.

Serves 4

Lamb tagine

1.5 kg (3 lb 5 oz) leg or shoulder
    lamb, cut into 2.5 cm (1 inch) pieces
3 garlic cloves, chopped
80 ml (1/3 cup) olive oil
2 teaspoons ground cumin
1 teaspoon ground ginger
1 teaspoon ground turmeric
1 teaspoon paprika
1/2 teaspoon ground cinnamon
2 onions, thinly sliced
580 ml (2 1/3 cups) beef stock
zest of 1/4 preserved lemon, rinsed,
    and cut into thin strips
425 g (15 oz) can chickpeas, drained
35 g (1 1/4 oz) cracked green olives
3 tablespoons chopped coriander
    (cilantro) leaves

Place the lamb in a non-metallic bowl, add the garlic, 2 tablespoons of the oil and the cumin, ginger, turmeric, paprika, cinnamon, 1/2 teaspoon ground black pepper and 1 teaspoon salt. Mix well to coat and leave to marinate for 1 hour.

Heat the remaining oil in a large saucepan, add the lamb in batches and brown the meat over high heat for 2–3 minutes. Remove from the pan. Add the onion and cook for 2 minutes, return the meat to the pan and add the beef stock. Reduce the heat and simmer, covered, for 1 hour. Add the lemon zest, chickpeas and olives and cook, uncovered, for a further 30 minutes, or until the meat is tender and the sauce reduced and thickened. Stir in the coriander. Serve in bowls with couscous.

Serves 6–8

Note: If you prefer, you can bake this lamb in the oven in a covered casserole dish. Preheat the oven to 190°C (375°F/Gas 5) and cook the tagine for about 1 hour, adding the lemon, chickpeas and olives after 40 minutes.

Chicken and corn pies

1 tablespoon olive oil
650 g (1 lb 7 oz) chicken thigh fillets,
  trimmed and cut into 1 cm (½ inch)
  pieces
1 tablespoon grated ginger
400 g (14 oz) oyster mushrooms,
  halved
3 corn cobs, kernels removed
125 ml (½ cup) chicken stock
2 tablespoons kecap manis
2 tablespoons cornflour (cornstarch)
30 g (1 cup) coriander (cilantro)
  leaves, chopped
6 sheets ready-rolled shortcrust
  pastry
milk, to glaze

Grease six metal pie tins measuring 9.5 cm (3¾ inches) on the base and 3 cm (1¼ inches) deep. Heat the oil in a large frying pan over high heat and add the chicken. Cook for 5 minutes, or until golden. Add the ginger, mushrooms and corn and cook for 5–6 minutes, or until the chicken is just cooked through. Add the stock and kecap manis.

Mix the cornflour with 2 tablespoons water in a small bowl or jug, then stir into the pan. Boil for 2 minutes before adding the coriander. Transfer to a bowl, cool a little, then refrigerate for 2 hours, or until cold.

Preheat the oven to moderate 180°C (350°F/Gas 4). Using a saucer to guide you, cut a 15 cm (6 inch) round from each sheet of shortcrust pastry and line the six pie tins. Fill the shells with the cooled filling, then cut out another six rounds large enough to make the lids. Top the pies with the lids, cut away any extra pastry and seal the edges with a fork. Decorate the pies with shapes cut from pastry scraps. Prick a few holes in the top of each pie, brush with a little milk and bake for 35 minutes, or until golden.

Makes 6

Ratatouille

4 tomatoes
2 tablespoons olive oil
1 large onion, diced
1 red capsicum (pepper), diced
1 yellow capsicum (pepper), diced
1 eggplant (aubergine), diced
2 zucchini (courgettes), diced
1 teaspoon tomato paste (purée)
$1/2$ teaspoon sugar
1 bay leaf
3 thyme sprigs
2 basil sprigs
1 garlic clove, crushed
1 tablespoon chopped parsley

Score a cross in the top of each tomato, plunge into boiling water for 20 seconds and then peel the skin away from the cross. Chop roughly.

Heat the oil in a frying pan. Add the onion and cook over low heat for 5 minutes. Add the capsicums and cook, stirring, for 4 minutes. Remove from the pan and set aside.

Fry the eggplant until lightly browned all over and then remove from the pan. Fry the zucchini until browned and then return the onion, capsicums and eggplant to the pan. Add the tomato paste, stir well and cook for 2 minutes. Add the tomato, sugar, bay leaf, thyme and basil, stir well, cover and cook for 15 minutes. Remove the bay leaf, thyme and basil.

Mix together the garlic and parsley and add to the ratatouille at the last minute. Stir and serve.

Serves 4

Welsh lamb pie

750 g (1lb 10 oz) boned lamb
  shoulder, cubed
90 g (³/₄ cup) plain (all-purpose) flour,
  seasoned
2 tablespoons olive oil
200 g (7 oz) bacon, finely chopped
2 garlic cloves, chopped
4 large leeks, sliced
1 large carrot, chopped
2 large potatoes, cut into 1 cm
  (½ inch) cubes
315 ml (1¼ cups) beef stock
1 bay leaf
2 teaspoons chopped flat-leaf (Italian)
  parsley
375 g (13 oz) puff pastry
1 egg, lightly beaten

Toss the meat in the seasoned flour and shake off the excess. Heat the oil in a large frying pan over medium heat. Cook the meat in batches for 4–5 minutes, or until well browned, then remove from the pan. Add the bacon and cook for 3 minutes. Add the garlic and leek and cook for about 5 minutes, or until the leek is soft.

Put the meat in a large saucepan, add the leek and bacon, carrot, potato, stock and bay leaf and bring to the boil, then reduce the heat, cover and simmer for 30 minutes. Uncover and simmer for 1 hour, or until the meat is cooked and the liquid has thickened. Season. Remove the bay leaf, stir in the parsley and set aside to cool.

Preheat the oven to 200°C (400°F/ Gas 6). Divide the filling among four 375 ml (1½ cups) pie dishes. Divide the pastry into four and roll each piece out between two sheets of baking paper until large enough to cover the pie. Remove the top sheet of paper and invert the pastry over the filling. Trim the edges and pinch to seal. Cut two slits in the top for steam to escape. Brush with egg and bake for 45 minutes, or until the pastry is crisp and golden.

Serves 6

Beef and red wine stew

1 kg (2 lb 4 oz) diced beef
30 g (¼ cup) plain (all-purpose) flour,
   seasoned
1 tablespoon oil
150 g (5½ oz) bacon, diced
8 bulb spring onions (scallions),
   greens trimmed to 2 cm (¾ inch)
200 g (7 oz) button mushrooms
500 ml (2 cups) red wine
2 tablespoons tomato paste (purée)
500 ml (2 cups) beef stock
bouquet garni (see Note)

Toss the beef in the flour until evenly coated, shaking off any excess. Heat the oil in a large saucepan over high heat. Cook the beef in three batches for about 3 minutes, or until well browned all over, adding a little extra oil as needed. Remove from the pan.

Add the bacon and cook for 2 minutes, or until browned. Remove with a slotted spoon and add to the beef. Add the spring onions and mushrooms and cook for 5 minutes, or until the onions are browned. Remove.

Slowly pour the red wine into the pan, scraping up any sediment from the bottom with a wooden spoon. Stir in the tomato paste and stock. Add the bouquet garni and return the beef, bacon and any juices. Bring to the boil, then reduce the heat and simmer for 45 minutes, then return the spring onions and mushrooms to the pan. Cook for 1 hour, or until the meat is tender and the sauce is glossy. Serve with steamed new potatoes or mash.

Serves 4

Note: To make a bouquet garni, wrap the green part of a leek around a bay leaf, a sprig of thyme, a sprig of parsley and celery leaves, and tie with string. The combination of herbs can be varied according to taste.

Beef, stout and potato pie

2 tablespoons olive oil
1.25 kg (2 lb 12 oz) chuck steak, cut
  into 3 cm (1 1/4 inch) cubes, excess
  fat trimmed
2 onions, sliced
2 rashers bacon, roughly chopped
4 garlic cloves, crushed
2 tablespoons plain (all-purpose) flour
440 ml (1 3/4 cups) stout
375 ml (1 1/2 cups) beef stock
1 1/2 tablespoons chopped thyme
2 large potatoes, thinly sliced
olive oil, for brushing

Heat 1 tablespoon of the oil over high heat in a large heavy-based flameproof casserole dish, add the beef in batches and cook, turning occasionally, for 5 minutes, or until the meat is nicely coloured. Remove from the dish. Reduce the heat to low, add the remaining oil to the dish, then cook the onion and bacon for 10 minutes, stirring occasionally. Add the garlic and cook for another minute. Return the beef to the dish.

Sprinkle the flour over the beef, cook for a minute, stirring, then gradually add the stout, stirring constantly. Add the stock, increase the heat to medium–high and bring to the boil. Stir in the thyme, season, then reduce the heat and simmer for 2 hours, or until the beef is tender and the mixture has thickened.

Preheat the oven to 200°C (400°F/ Gas 6). Lightly grease a 1.25 litre (5 cup) ovenproof dish and pour in the beef mixture. Arrange potato slices in a single overlapping layer over the top to cover the meat. Brush over the top with olive oil and sprinkle with salt. Bake for 30–40 minutes, or until the potato is golden.

Serves 6

Tuna bake

200 g (7 oz) short curly pasta such as
  cotelli or fusilli
4 eggs, hard-boiled and roughly
  chopped
4 spring onions (scallions), finely
  chopped
1 tablespoon chopped dill
1 tablespoon lemon juice
115 g (4 oz) butter
3 teaspoons madras curry powder
50 g (1/3 cup) plain (all-purpose) flour
375 ml (1 1/2 cups) milk
375 ml (1 1/2 cups) cream
175 g (6 oz) whole-egg mayonnaise
3 x 210 g (7 1/2 oz) cans tuna, drained
160 g (2 cups) fresh white
  breadcrumbs
1 garlic clove, crushed
1 tablespoon finely chopped flat-leaf
  (Italian) parsley
2 tablespoons grated Parmesan
  cheese

Preheat the oven to 180°C (350°F/
Gas 4). Cook the pasta in a large
saucepan of rapidly boiling salted
water until *al dente*. Drain well. Lightly
grease a 2 litre (8 cup) ovenproof dish.
Combine the egg, spring onion, dill
and lemon juice and season.

Melt 60 g (2 1/4 oz) of the butter in a
saucepan, add the curry powder and
cook for 30 seconds. Stir in the flour
and cook for 1 minute, or until
foaming. Remove from the heat,
gradually stir in the milk and cream,
then return to low heat and stir
constantly until the sauce boils and
thickens. Reduce to a simmer for
2 minutes, then stir in the mayonnaise.
Combine the sauce, cooked pasta,
tuna and egg mixture and spoon into
the prepared dish.

Melt the remaining butter in a frying
pan, add the breadcrumbs and garlic
and cook, stirring, for 1 minute, or
until the breadcrumbs are golden and
coated in butter. Stir in the parsley
and grated Parmesan and then
sprinkle over the tuna mixture. Bake
for 15–20 minutes, or until golden and
heated through.

Serves 6

Orzo and Greek cheese bake

415 g (2 cups) orzo (rice-shaped
  pasta)
60 g (2¼ oz) butter
6 spring onions (scallions), chopped
450 g (1 lb) English spinach, stems
  removed, rinsed well and chopped
2 tablespoons plain (all-purpose) flour
1.25 litres (5 cups) milk
250 g (9 oz) kefalotyri cheese, grated
  (see Note)
250 g (9 oz) marinated feta cheese,
  well drained
3 tablespoons chopped dill

Preheat the oven to 190°C (375°F/
Gas 5). Cook the pasta in a large
saucepan of boiling salted water until
al dente. Drain well, then return to the
pan. Heat 20 g (¾ oz) of the butter in
a large saucepan over high heat and
cook the spring onion for 30 seconds.
Add the spinach and stir for 1 minute.
Season and stir into the orzo.

Put the remaining butter in the pan in
which the spinach was cooked. Melt
over low heat, then stir in the flour
and cook for 1 minute, or until pale
and foaming. Remove from the heat
and gradually stir in the milk. Return
to the heat and stir constantly for
5 minutes, or until the sauce boils
and thickens. Add two-thirds of the
kefalotyri and all of the feta and stir for
2 minutes, or until melted and well
mixed. Remove from the heat and stir
in the dill.

Combine the pasta mixture with the
cheese sauce, season and pour into a
greased 2.5 litre (10 cup) ovenproof
ceramic dish. Sprinkle the remaining
cheese over the top and bake for
15 minutes, or until golden.

Serves 6

Note: Kefalotyri is a hard Greek sheep's
or goat's milk cheese. Parmesan or
pecorino cheese can be substituted.

Braised lamb shanks in rich tomato sauce

2 tablespoons olive oil
1 large red onion, sliced
4 French-trimmed lamb shanks (about
   250 g/9 oz each)
2 garlic cloves, crushed
400 g (14 oz) can peeled chopped
   tomatoes
125 ml (½ cup) red wine
2 teaspoons chopped rosemary
150 g (1 cup) instant polenta
   (cornmeal)
50 g (1¾ oz) butter
50 g (½ cup) grated Parmesan
   cheese

Preheat the oven to 160°C (315°F/ Gas 2–3). Heat the oil in a 4 litre (16 cup) flameproof casserole dish over medium heat and cook the onion for 3–4 minutes, or until soft and translucent. Add the lamb shanks and cook for 2–3 minutes, or until lightly browned. Add the garlic, tomato and wine, then bring to the boil and cook for 3–4 minutes. Stir in the rosemary. Season with ¼ teaspoon each of salt and pepper.

Cover, transfer to the oven and cook for 2 hours. Remove the lid, return to the oven and simmer for a further 15 minutes, or until the lamb just starts to fall off the bone. Check periodically that the sauce is not too dry, adding water if needed.

About 20 minutes before serving, bring 1 litre (4 cups) water to the boil in a saucepan. Add the polenta in a thin stream, whisking continuously, then reduce the heat to very low. Simmer for 8–10 minutes, or until thick and coming away from the side of the saucepan. Stir in the butter and Parmesan. To serve, spoon the polenta onto serving plates, top with the shanks and a little sauce from the casserole over the shanks.

Serves 4

Shellfish stew

16 mussels
12 large prawns (shrimp)
435 ml (1³/₄ cups) cider or dry white
  wine
50 g (1³/₄ oz) butter
1 garlic clove, crushed
2 shallots, finely chopped
2 celery stalks, finely chopped
1 large leek, white part only, thinly
  sliced
250 g (9 oz) small chestnut
  mushrooms, sliced
1 bay leaf
300 g (10¹/₂ oz) salmon fillet, skinned
  and cut into chunks
400 g (14 oz) sole fillet, skinned and
  cut into thick strips widthways
300 ml (10¹/₂ fl oz) thick
  (double/heavy) cream
3 tablespoons finely chopped parsley

Scrub the mussels and remove their beards. Throw away any that are open and don't close when tapped on the bench. Peel and devein the prawns.

Pour the cider into a large saucepan and bring to a simmer. Add the mussels, cover the pan and cook for 3–5 minutes, shaking the pan every now and then. Place a fine sieve over a bowl, tip in the mussels, then transfer them to a plate, throwing away any that haven't opened. Strain the cooking liquid again through the sieve.

Add the butter to the cleaned saucepan and melt over moderate heat. Add the garlic, shallot, celery and leek and cook for 7–10 minutes, or until the vegetables are just soft. Add the mushrooms and cook for a further 4–5 minutes until softened. While the vegetables are cooking, remove the mussels from their shells.

Add the strained liquid to the vegetables in the saucepan, add the bay leaf and bring to a simmer. Add the salmon, sole and prawns and cook for 3–4 minutes until the fish is opaque and the prawns are pink. Stir in the cream and cooked mussels and simmer for 2 minutes. Season and stir in the parsley.

Serves 6

Moussaka

2 large eggplants (aubergines),
    about 800 g (1 lb 12 oz), sliced
    lengthways into 1.5 cm (⅝ inch)
    thick pieces
1 tablespoon olive oil
1 large onion, chopped
1 garlic clove, crushed
500 g (1 lb 2 oz) minced (ground) beef
125 ml (½ cup) red wine
125 g (½ cup) tomato paste (purée)
pinch of ground cinnamon
2 teaspoons chopped oregano
3 tablespoons chopped flat-leaf
    (Italian) parsley
2 tablespoons grated Parmesan
    cheese
2 tablespoons dry breadcrumbs

Sauce
20 g (¾ oz) butter
40 g (⅓ cup) plain (all-purpose) flour
500 ml (2 cups) milk
pinch of ground nutmeg
1 tablespoon grated Parmesan
    cheese

Preheat the oven to 200°C (400°F/ Gas 6). Spread the eggplant slices on two foil-lined baking sheets and brush both sides using a little of the oil. Bake for 10 minutes, turn the slices and bake for 10 minutes more. Cool.

Heat the remaining oil in a large pan. Add the onion and garlic and cook for 4–5 minutes. Increase the heat to high and brown the mince for 5 minutes. Stir in the wine, tomato paste, cinnamon, oregano and a quarter of the parsley. Season. Reduce to a simmer, stirring occasionally, for 15–20 minutes. Remove from the heat.

To make the sauce, melt the butter in a small saucepan. Stir in the flour and cook over low heat for 2–3 minutes. Slowly whisk in the milk, cooking for 6–8 minutes until thickened. Remove from the heat and add the nutmeg, Parmesan and ½ teaspoon salt.

Grease an 18 x 28 cm (7 x 11 inch) rectangular casserole dish. Line the base with a layer of eggplant, then top with the mince. Cover with the remaining eggplant, then pour over the sauce. Mix together the Parmesan, breadcrumbs and remaining parsley, season, then sprinkle over the top. Bake for 30 minutes, or until golden.

Serves 4–6

Steak and kidney pie

60 g (½ cup) plain (all-purpose) flour,
seasoned
1.5 kg (3 lb 5 oz) chuck steak, cut
into 2 cm (¾ inch) cubes
1 ox kidney (500 g/1 lb 2 oz), cut into
2 cm (¾ inch) cubes
2 tablespoons olive oil
2 onions, chopped
125 g (4½ oz) button mushrooms,
quartered___
40 g (1½ oz) butter
250 ml (1 cup) beef or veal stock
185 ml (¾ cup) stout
2 tablespoons Worcestershire sauce
1 tablespoon anchovy essence
1 tablespoon chopped flat-leaf (Italian)
parsley
600 g (1 lb 5 oz) puff pastry
1 egg, lightly beaten

Place the flour in a bowl. Toss the steak and kidney pieces through the flour and shake off any excess. Heat the oil in a large pan over medium heat, add the onion and cook for 5 minutes. Add the mushrooms and cook for 5 minutes. Remove from the pan.

Melt a third of the butter in the pan, add a third of the beef and kidney and cook over medium heat, turning occasionally, for 5 minutes, or until brown. Remove and repeat twice with the remaining butter, beef and kidney. Return all the meat to the saucepan, add the stock and stout, stir and bring slowly to boil. Reduce the heat and simmer for 2 hours. Remove from the heat, leave to cool, then add the onion and mushrooms, Worcestershire sauce, anchovy essence and parsley.

Preheat the oven to 180°C (350°F/Gas 4). Place the filling into a ceramic pie dish measuring 20 cm (8 inches) on the base and 4 cm (1½ inches) deep. Roll out the pastry between two sheets of baking paper to fit the top of the pie dish. Moisten the rim of the dish with milk and place the pastry over the filling. Press firmly into place and brush with egg. Decorate with pastry scraps, brush with egg and bake for 40–45 minutes until golden.

Serves 6

Rich cheese macaroni

450 g (1 lb) elbow macaroni
40 g (1½ oz) butter
300 ml (10½ fl oz) cream
125 g (4½ oz) fontina cheese, sliced
125 g (4½ oz) provolone cheese,
  grated
100 g (3½ oz) Gruyère cheese, grated
125 g (4½ oz) blue castello cheese,
  crumbled
40 g (½ cup) fresh white
  breadcrumbs
25 g (¼ cup) grated Parmesan
  cheese

Preheat the oven to 180°C (350°F/ Gas 4). Cook the pasta in a large saucepan of boiling salted water until *al dente*. Drain and keep warm.

Melt half the butter in a large saucepan. Add the cream and, when just coming to the boil, add the fontina, provolone, Gruyère and blue castello cheeses, stirring constantly over low heat for 3 minutes, or until melted. Season with salt and ground white pepper. Add the pasta to the cheese mixture and mix well.

Spoon the mixture into a greased shallow 2 litre (8 cup) ovenproof dish. Sprinkle with the breadcrumbs mixed with the Parmesan, dot with the remaining cubed butter and bake for 25 minutes, or until the top is golden and crisp. Serve with a salad.

Serves 4

Osso buco with tomatoes

10 pieces veal shank, about 4 cm
  (1½ inch) thick
plain (all-purpose) flour, seasoned with
  salt and pepper
60 ml (¼ cup) olive oil
60 g (2¼ oz) butter
1 garlic clove
1 small carrot, finely chopped
1 large onion, finely chopped
½ celery stalk, finely chopped
250 ml (1 cup) dry white wine
375 ml (1½ cups) veal or chicken
  stock
400 g (14 oz) can chopped tomatoes
bouquet garni

Tie each piece of veal shank around its girth to secure the flesh, then dust with the seasoned flour. Heat the oil, butter and garlic in a large heavy saucepan big enough to hold the shanks in a single layer. Put the shanks in the saucepan and cook for 12–15 minutes until well browned. Remove the shanks from the pan and set aside. Discard the garlic.

Add the carrot, onion and celery to the pan and cook over moderate heat for 5–6 minutes, without browning. Increase the heat to high, add the wine and cook for 2–3 minutes. Add the stock, tomatoes and bouquet garni. Season with salt and pepper.

Return the veal shanks to the pan, standing them up in a single layer. Cover the pan, reduce the heat and simmer for 1 hour, or until the meat is tender and you can cut it with a fork.

If you prefer a thicker sauce, remove the veal shanks and increase the heat. Boil the sauce until reduced and thickened, then return the veal to the saucepan. Discard the bouquet garni, and taste for salt and pepper. If desired, serve with mashed potato.

Serves 4

Hoisin beef stew

1 1/2 tablespoons peanut oil
1 kg (2 lb 4 oz) stewing beef (such
    as chuck), cut into 3 cm (1 1/4 inch)
    cubes
1 tablespoon finely chopped ginger
1 tablespoon finely chopped garlic
1 litre (4 cups) good-quality beef
    stock
80 ml (1/3 cup) Chinese rice wine
80 ml (1/3 cup) hoisin sauce
5 cm (2 inch) piece cassia bark
1 piece dried tangerine peel
1 star anise
1 teaspoon Sichuan peppercorns,
    lightly crushed
2 teaspoons soft brown sugar
300 g (10 1/2 oz) daikon, cut into
    3 cm (1 1/4 inch) chunks
3 spring onions (scallions), cut into
    3 cm (1 1/4 inch) lengths, plus extra,
    to garnish
50 g (1 3/4 oz) sliced bamboo shoots
a few drops sesame oil (optional)

Heat a wok until very hot, add the peanut oil and swirl to coat the side. Stir-fry the beef in four batches for 1–2 minutes for each batch, or until the meat is browned all over. Remove from the wok.

Add the ginger and garlic to the wok and stir-fry for a few seconds. Add the stock, rice wine, hoisin sauce, cassia bark, tangerine peel, star anise, Sichuan peppercorns, sugar, daikon and 875 ml (3 1/2 cups) water, then return the beef to the wok.

Bring to the boil, skimming any scum that forms on the surface, then reduce to a simmer and cook, stirring occasionally, for 1 1/2 hours, or until the beef is tender and the sauce has thickened slightly. Add the spring onion and bamboo shoots 5 minutes before the end of the cooking time. Stir in a few drops of sesame oil, if desired, and garnish with extra spring onion. Serve with rice.

Serves 6

Note: You can remove the star anise, cassia bark and tangerine peel before serving or leave them in the serving dish for presentation.

Pork sausage, soya bean and tomato casserole

325 g (1½ cups) dried soya beans,
  soaked in cold water for at least
  8 hours, or overnight
8 thin pork sausages (550 g/1 lb 4 oz)
2 tablespoons oil
1 red onion, chopped
4 garlic cloves, chopped
1 large carrot, diced
1 celery stalk, diced
2 x 400 g (14 oz) cans chopped
  tomatoes
1 tablespoon tomato paste (purée)
250 ml (1 cup) white wine
2 thyme sprigs
1 teaspoon dried oregano leaves
1 tablespoon oregano, chopped

Drain the soya beans, place in a large saucepan and cover with fresh water. Bring to the boil, then reduce the heat and slowly simmer for 1¼ –2 hours — keep the beans covered with water during cooking. Drain. Prick the sausages all over and then cook in a frying pan for 10 minutes, or until browned. Drain on paper towels.

Heat the oil in a 3.5 litre (14 cup) flameproof casserole dish. Add the onion and garlic and cook on the stovetop over medium heat for 5 minutes. Add the carrot and celery. Cook, stirring, for 5 minutes. Stir in the tomato, tomato paste, wine, thyme and dried oregano and bring to the boil. Reduce to a simmer, stirring often, for 10 minutes, or until the liquid has reduced and thickened slightly.

Preheat the oven to 160°C (315°F/ Gas 2–3). Add the sausages, beans and 250 ml (1 cup) water to the casserole dish. Bake, covered, for 2 hours. Stir occasionally, adding more water if necessary to keep the beans just covered.

Return the dish to the stovetop, skim off any fat, then reduce the liquid until thickened slightly. Remove the thyme sprigs and stir through the oregano.

Serves 4

Slow-cooked lamb shanks with soft polenta

60 ml (¼ cup) olive oil
8 French-trimmed lamb shanks
30 g (¼ cup) seasoned flour
2 onions, sliced
3 garlic cloves, crushed
1 celery stalk, cut into 2.5 cm (1 inch)
    lengths
2 long thin carrots, cut into 3 cm
    (1¼ inch) chunks
2 parsnips, peeled and cut into 3 cm
    (1¼ inch) chunks
250 ml (1 cup) red wine
750 ml (3 cups) chicken stock
250 ml (1 cup) tomato passata
1 bay leaf
1 thyme sprig, plus extra, to garnish
zest of half an orange (without pith),
    cut into thick strips
1 parsley sprig

Polenta
500 ml (2 cups) chicken stock
150 g (1 cup) fine instant polenta
    (cornmeal)
50 g (1¾ oz) butter
pinch paprika, for sprinkling

Preheat the oven to 160°C (315°F/ Gas 2–3). Heat the oil in a large heavy-based flameproof casserole dish, big enough to fit the shanks in a single layer. Lightly dust the shanks with seasoned flour, then brown them in batches on the stovetop. Remove from the dish. Add the onion, reduce the heat and cook for 3 minutes. Stir in the garlic, celery, carrot and parsnip, add the wine and simmer for 1 minute, then return the shanks to the casserole dish. Add the stock, tomato passata, bay leaf, thyme, orange zest and parsley. Cover and bake for 2 hours.

To make the polenta, place the stock and 500 ml (2 cups) water in a large saucepan and bring to the boil. Gradually stir in the polenta using a wooden spoon. Reduce the heat and simmer over low heat, stirring often, for 5–6 minutes, or until the mixture thickens and starts to leave the side of the pan. Remove from the heat, stir in the butter and season. Spoon into a warm dish and sprinkle with paprika.

Remove the shanks from the pan and arrange on a warm serving platter. Discard the herbs and zest, then spoon the vegetables and gravy over the shanks. Garnish with the thyme sprigs. Serve with the soft polenta.

Serves 4

Chicken casserole with mustard and tarragon

60 ml (¼ cup) olive oil
1 kg (2 lb 4 oz) chicken thigh fillets,
    halved, then quartered
1 onion, finely chopped
1 leek, sliced
1 garlic clove, finely chopped
350 g (12 oz) button mushrooms,
    sliced
½ teaspoon dried tarragon
375 ml (1½ cups) chicken stock
185 ml (¾ cup) cream
2 teaspoons lemon juice
2 teaspoons Dijon mustard

Preheat the oven to 180°C (350°F/ Gas 4). Heat 1 tablespoon of the oil in a flameproof casserole dish over medium heat, and cook the chicken in two batches for 6–7 minutes each, or until golden. Remove from the dish.

Add the remaining oil to the casserole dish and cook the onion, leek and garlic over medium heat for 5 minutes, or until soft. Add the mushrooms and cook for 5–7 minutes, or until they are soft and browned and most of the liquid has evaporated. Add the tarragon, chicken stock, cream, lemon juice and mustard, bring to the boil and cook for 2 minutes. Return the chicken pieces to the dish and season well. Cover.

Place the casserole in the oven and cook for 1 hour, or until the sauce has reduced and thickened. Season with salt and pepper and serve with potatoes and a green salad.

Serves 4–6

Veal Marsala

4 pieces (500 g/1 lb 2 oz) veal
  schnitzel
plain (all-purpose) flour, seasoned
50 g (1³/₄ oz) butter
1 tablespoon oil
185 ml (³/₄ cup) dry Marsala
3 teaspoons cream
30 g (1 oz) butter, chopped, extra

Using a meat mallet or the heel of your hand, flatten the schnitzel pieces to 5 mm (¼ inch) thick. Dust the veal in the flour, shaking off any excess. Heat the butter and oil in a large frying pan and cook the veal over medium–high heat for 1–2 minutes on each side, or until almost cooked through. Remove and keep warm.

Add the Marsala to the pan and bring to the boil, scraping the base of the pan to loosen any sediment. Reduce the heat and simmer for 1–2 minutes, or until slightly reduced. Add the cream and simmer for 2 minutes, then whisk in the extra butter until the sauce thickens slightly. Return the veal to the pan and simmer for 1 minute, or until the meat is warmed through. Serve immediately. Delicious with a creamy garlic mash and a tossed green salad.

Serves 4

Note: Purchase veal that is pale in colour and free of sinew. Sinew will make the meat tough.

Fried beef with potato, peas and ginger

oil, for deep-frying
1 potato, cut into small cubes
2.5 cm (1 inch) piece of ginger
500 g (1 lb 2 oz) beef rump steak,
   thinly sliced
3 garlic cloves, crushed
1 teaspoon ground black pepper
2 tablespoons oil, extra
2 onions, sliced in rings
60 ml (1/4 cup) beef stock
2 tablespoons tomato paste (purée)
1/2 tablespoon soy sauce
1 teaspoon chilli powder
3 tablespoons lemon juice
3 tomatoes, chopped
50 g (1/3 cup) fresh or frozen peas

Fill a deep heavy-based saucepan one-third full with oil and heat to 180°C (350°F), or until a cube of bread dropped in the oil browns in 15 seconds. Deep-fry the potato cubes until golden brown. Drain on paper towels.

Pound the ginger using a mortar and pestle, or grate with a fine grater into a bowl. Put the ginger into a piece of muslin, twist it up tightly and squeeze out all the juice (you will need about 1 tablespoon).

Put the steak in a bowl, add the garlic, pepper and ginger juice and toss well. Heat the oil and fry the beef quickly in batches over high heat. Keep each batch warm as you remove it. Reduce the heat, fry the onions until golden, then remove.

Put the stock, tomato paste, soy sauce, chilli powder and lemon juice in the saucepan and cook over medium heat until reduced. Add the fried onion, cook for 3 minutes, add the chopped tomato and the peas, then stir well and cook for 1 minute. Add the beef and potato and toss well until heated through.

Serves 4

Beef stroganoff

400 g (14 oz) beef fillet, cut into
   1 x 5 cm (1/2 x 2 inch) strips
2 tablespoons plain (all-purpose) flour
50 g (1 3/4 oz) butter
1 onion, thinly sliced
1 garlic clove, crushed
250 g (9 oz) small Swiss brown
   mushrooms, sliced
60 ml (1/4 cup) brandy
250 ml (1 cup) beef stock
1 1/2 tablespoons tomato paste (purée)
185 g (3/4 cup) sour cream
1 tablespoon chopped flat-leaf (Italian)
   parsley

Dust the beef strips in flour, shaking off any excess.

Melt half the butter in a large frying pan and cook the meat in small batches for 1–2 minutes, or until seared all over. Remove. Add the remaining butter to the pan and cook the onion and garlic over medium heat for 2–3 minutes, or until they soften. Add the mushrooms and cook for 2–3 minutes.

Pour in the brandy and simmer until nearly all of the liquid has evaporated, then stir in the beef stock and tomato paste. Cook for 5 minutes to reduce the liquid slightly. Return the beef strips to the pan with any juices and stir in the sour cream. Simmer for 1 minute, or until the sauce thickens slightly. Season with salt and freshly ground black pepper.

Garnish with the chopped parsley and serve immediately with fettucine or steamed rice.

Serves 4

Irish stew

20 g (³/₄ oz) butter
1 tablespoon vegetable oil
8 lamb neck chops, trimmed
4 rashers bacon, cut into strips
1 teaspoon plain (all-purpose) flour
600 g (1 lb 5 oz) potatoes, peeled and
  cut into thick slices
3 carrots, cut into thick slices
1 onion, cut into 16 wedges
1 small leek, cut into thick slices
150 g (5½ oz) savoy cabbage, thinly
  sliced
500 ml (2 cups) beef stock
2 tablespoons finely chopped flat-leaf
  (Italian) parsley

Heat the butter and oil in a flameproof casserole dish or a large heavy-based saucepan over high heat. Add the chops and cook for 1–2 minutes on each side, or until browned, then remove from the dish. Add the bacon and cook for 2–3 minutes, or until crisp. Remove with a slotted spoon, leaving the drippings in the dish.

Sprinkle the flour into the dish and stir to combine. Remove from the heat and layer half the potato, carrot, onion, leek, cabbage and bacon in the base of the dish. Arrange the chops in a single layer over the bacon and cover with layers of the remaining vegetables and bacon.

Pour in enough of the stock to cover, then bring to the boil over high heat. Reduce the heat, cover, and simmer for 1½ hours, or until the meat is very tender and the sauce is slightly reduced. Season well with salt and freshly ground black pepper and serve sprinkled with the parsley.

Serves 4

Beef cooked in ragù

1.5 kg (3 lb 5 oz) piece of beef, such
as top rump or silverside
60 g (2¼ oz) pork fat, cut into small
thin pieces
30 g (1 oz) butter
3 tablespoons olive oil
pinch of cayenne pepper
2 garlic cloves, finely chopped
2 onions, finely chopped
2 carrots, finely chopped
1 celery stalk, finely chopped
½ red capsicum (pepper), finely
chopped
3 leeks, sliced
185 ml (¾ cup) red wine
1 tablespoon tomato purée
375 ml (1½ cups) beef stock
200 ml (7 fl oz) tomato passata
8 basil leaves, torn into pieces
½ teaspoon finely chopped oregano
leaves or ¼ teaspoon dried oregano
2 tablespoons finely chopped parsley
60 ml (¼ cup) thick (double/heavy)
cream

Make deep incisions all over the piece
of beef using the point of a sharp
knife, then push a piece of pork fat
into each incision.

Heat the butter and olive oil in a large
casserole dish and brown the beef for
10–12 minutes, until it is browned all
over. Season with salt and add the
cayenne, garlic, onion, carrot, celery,
capsicum and leek. Cook over
moderate heat for 10 minutes until the
vegetables are lightly browned.

Increase the heat, add the wine and
boil until it has evaporated. Stir in the
tomato purée, then add the stock.
Simmer for 30 minutes. Add the
tomato passata, basil and oregano
and season with pepper. Cover the
casserole dish and cook for 1 hour, or
until the beef is tender.

Remove the beef from the dish and
allow to rest for 10 minutes before
carving. Taste the sauce for salt and
pepper and then stir in the parsley
and cream.

Serves 6

Note: This dish can be both starter
and main course in one pot. Serve the
ragù on spaghetti or bucatini as a first
course, and the beef with vegetables
or a salad for the main.

Curried sausages

9 thick beef or pork sausages
1 tablespoon vegetable oil
20 g ($^3/_4$ oz) butter
2 teaspoons grated ginger
3 garlic cloves, crushed
2 large onions, sliced
3 teaspoons curry powder
1 teaspoon garam masala
2 teaspoons tomato paste (purée)
1 tablespoon plain (all-purpose) flour
625 ml (2½ cups) hot chicken stock
2 bay leaves

Place the sausages in a saucepan, cover with cold water and bring to the boil. Lower the heat and simmer for 3 minutes. Remove from the heat and allow the sausages to cool in the water, then drain, pat dry, and cut into 2 cm ($^3/_4$ inch) pieces.

Heat the oil in a large frying pan over high heat and cook the sausages for 2–3 minutes, or until golden all over. Drain on paper towels.

Using the same pan, melt the butter, then add the ginger, garlic and onion. Cook over medium heat for about 5 minutes, or until the onion is soft and golden. Add the curry powder and garam masala and cook for 1 minute, or until fragrant. Stir in the tomato paste and cook for 1 minute, then add the flour. Stir to combine, then gradually pour in the stock, taking care that no lumps form. Bring to a simmer, add the bay leaves and the sausages and cook over low heat for 15 minutes, or until thickened. Season and serve with mashed potato.

Serves 6

Pasta

Pasta with tomato and basil sauce

500 g (1 lb 2 oz) penne rigate
80 ml (⅓ cup) extra virgin olive oil
4 garlic cloves, crushed
4 anchovy fillets, finely chopped
2 small red chillies, seeded and finely
  chopped
6 large, vine-ripened tomatoes,
  peeled, seeded and diced
80 ml (⅓ cup) white wine
1 tablespoon tomato paste (purée)
2 teaspoons sugar
2 tablespoons finely chopped flat-leaf
  (Italian) parsley
3 tablespoons shredded basil

Cook the pasta in a saucepan of boiling salted water until *al dente*. Drain well.

Meanwhile, heat the oil in a frying pan and cook the garlic for 30 seconds. Stir in the anchovy and chilli and cook for a further 30 seconds. Add the tomato and cook for 2 minutes over high heat. Add the wine, tomato paste and sugar and simmer, covered, for 10 minutes, or until thickened.

Toss the tomato sauce through the pasta with the herbs. Season and serve with grated Parmesan, if desired.

Serves 4

Genovese pesto sauce

Pesto
2 garlic cloves
50 g (1/3 cup) pine nuts
125 g (4½ oz) basil, stems removed
150–185 ml (5–6 fl oz) extra virgin
   olive oil
50 g (1¾ oz) Parmesan cheese, finely
   grated, plus extra, to serve

500 g (1 lb 2 oz) trenette or spaghetti
   (see Note)
175 g (6 oz) green beans, trimmed
175 g (6 oz) small potatoes, very
   thinly sliced

Put the garlic and pine nuts in a food processor and process until finely ground (or use a mortar and pestle to do this). Add the basil and then drizzle in the olive oil a little at a time while pounding or processing. When you have a thick purée, stop adding the oil. Season and mix in the Parmesan.

Bring a large saucepan of salted water to the boil. Add the pasta, green beans and potatoes, stirring well to prevent the pasta from sticking together. Cook until the pasta is *al dente* (the vegetables should be cooked by this time), then drain, reserving a little of the water.

Return the pasta and vegetables to the saucepan, add the pesto, and mix well. If necessary, add some of the reserved water to loosen the pasta. Season and serve immediately with the extra Parmesan.

Serves 4

Note: Traditionally, pesto sauce is served with trenette pasta, green beans and potatoes, but you can leave out the vegetables if you prefer or use spaghetti.

Penne with mushroom and herb sauce

2 tablespoons olive oil
500 g (1 lb 2 oz) button mushrooms, sliced
2 garlic cloves, crushed
2 teaspoons chopped marjoram
125 ml (1/2 cup) dry white wine
80 ml (1/3 cup) cream
375 g (13 oz) penne
1 tablespoon lemon juice
1 teaspoon finely grated lemon zest
2 tablespoons chopped parsley
50 g (1/2 cup) grated Parmesan cheese

Heat the oil in a large heavy-based frying pan over high heat. Add the mushrooms and cook for 3 minutes, stirring constantly to prevent the mushrooms from burning. Add the garlic and marjoram and cook for a further 2 minutes.

Add the white wine to the pan, reduce the heat and simmer for 5 minutes, or until nearly all the liquid has evaporated. Stir in the cream and cook over low heat for 5 minutes, or until the sauce has thickened.

Meanwhile, cook the penne in a large saucepan of boiling salted water until *al dente*. Drain.

Add the lemon juice, zest, parsley and half the Parmesan to the sauce. Season to taste with salt and freshly ground black pepper. Toss the penne through the sauce and sprinkle with the remaining Parmesan.

Serves 4

Ricotta agnolotti with salmon and capers

125 ml (1/2 cup) olive oil
100 g (3 1/2 oz) capers, patted dry
500 g (1 lb 2 oz) salmon fillets,
   skinned
625 g (1 lb 6 oz) ricotta agnolotti
150 g (5 1/2 oz) butter
1 1/2 teaspoons grated lemon zest
2 tablespoons lemon juice
3 tablespoons chopped parsley

Heat half the oil in a small frying pan and cook the capers over high heat for 3–4 minutes, or until golden and crispy. Drain on paper towels.

Season the salmon on both sides with salt and pepper. Heat the remaining oil in a non-stick frying pan and cook the salmon for 2–3 minutes each side, or until just cooked through but still pink in the centre. Remove from the pan and keep warm. Gently break into flakes with your fingers, being careful to remove any bones.

Cook the pasta in a large saucepan of boiling salted water until *al dente*. Drain and return to the pan to keep warm. Heat the butter in a frying pan over low heat for 5 minutes, or until golden. Add the lemon zest, lemon juice and parsley. Top the pasta with the flaked salmon and pour on the brown butter. Scatter with the capers and serve immediately.

Serves 4

Creamy tomato and prawn pasta

400 g (14 oz) dried egg tagliatelle
1 tablespoon olive oil
3 garlic cloves, finely chopped
20 medium raw prawns (shrimp), peeled and deveined, with tails intact
550 g (1 lb 4 oz) Roma (plum) tomatoes, diced
2 tablespoons thinly sliced basil
125 ml (½ cup) white wine
80 ml (⅓ cup) cream
basil leaves, to garnish

Cook the pasta in a large saucepan of boiling salted water until *al dente*. Drain and keep warm, reserving 2 tablespoons of the cooking water.

Meanwhile, heat the oil and garlic in a large frying pan over low heat for 1–2 minutes. Increase the heat to medium, add the prawns and cook for 3–5 minutes, stirring frequently until cooked. Remove the prawns and keep warm.

Add the tomato and sliced basil and stir for 3 minutes, or until the tomato is soft. Pour in the wine and cream, bring to the boil and simmer for 2 minutes.

Purée the sauce in a blender, return to the pan, then add the reserved pasta water and bring to a simmer. Stir in the prawns until heated through. Toss through the pasta and serve garnished with the basil leaves.

Serves 4

Orecchiette with spiced pumpkin and yoghurt

1 kg (2 lb 4 oz) pumpkin or butternut
   pumpkin (squash), cut into 2 cm
   ($^3/_4$ inch) cubes
80 ml ($^1/_3$ cup) olive oil
500 g (1 lb 2 oz) orecchiette (see
   Note)
2 garlic cloves, crushed
1 teaspoon dried chilli flakes
1 teaspoon coriander seeds, crushed
1 tablespoon cumin seeds, crushed
185 g ($^3/_4$ cup) thick natural yoghurt
3 tablespoons chopped coriander
   (cilantro) leaves

Preheat the oven to 200°C (400°F/
Gas 6). Toss the pumpkin cubes in
2 tablespoons of the oil, place in a
roasting tin and cook for 30 minutes,
or until golden and crisp, tossing
halfway through.

Meanwhile, cook the pasta in a large
saucepan of boiling salted water until
al dente. Drain and return to the pan.

Heat the remaining oil in a saucepan.
Add the garlic, chilli, coriander and
cumin and cook for 30 seconds, or
until fragrant. Toss the spice mix and
pumpkin through the pasta, then stir
in the yoghurt and coriander and
season to taste with salt and freshly
ground black pepper. Divide among
serving bowls.

Serves 6

Note: Orecchiette means 'little ears'
in Italian, and the name of the pasta
is a literal description of the shape —
although some brands look more like
curls than ears. If unavailable, use
conchiglie or cavatelli.

Tagliatelle with tuna, capers and rocket

350 g (12 oz) fresh tagliatelle
3 garlic cloves, crushed
1 teaspoon finely grated lemon zest
80 ml (1/3 cup) extra virgin olive oil
500 g (1 lb 2 oz) tuna, cut into 1.5 cm
  (5/8 inch) cubes
200 g (7 oz) rocket (arugula) leaves,
  washed, dried and roughly chopped
4 tablespoons baby capers in salt,
  rinsed and squeezed dry
60 ml (1/4 cup) lemon juice
2 tablespoons finely chopped flat-leaf
  (Italian) parsley

Cook the pasta in a saucepan of boiling salted water until *al dente*.

Meanwhile, put the garlic, lemon zest and 1 tablespoon of the oil in a bowl with the tuna and gently mix. Season.

Heat a frying pan over high heat and sear the tuna for 30 seconds on each side. Add the rocket and capers and gently stir for 1 minute, or until the rocket has just wilted. Pour in the lemon juice and then remove from the heat.

Add the remaining oil to the hot pasta along with the tuna mixture and parsley. Season to taste and gently toss. Serve immediately.

Serves 4

Pasta carbonara

400 g (14 oz) penne
1 tablespoon olive oil
200 g (7 oz) piece pancetta or bacon,
  cut into long thin strips
6 egg yolks
185 ml (3/4 cup) thick (double/heavy)
  cream
75 g (3/4 cup) grated Parmesan
  cheese

Cook the pasta in a saucepan of boiling salted water until *al dente*.

Meanwhile, heat the oil in a frying pan and cook the pancetta over high heat for 6 minutes, or until crisp and golden. Remove with a slotted spoon and drain on paper towels.

Beat the egg yolks, cream and the Parmesan together in a bowl and season generously. Return the freshly cooked and drained pasta to its saucepan and pour the egg mixture over the pasta, tossing gently. Add the pancetta, then return the pan to very low heat and cook for 30–60 seconds, or until the sauce thickens and coats the pasta. Season with pepper and serve immediately.

Serves 4–6

Note: Be careful not to cook the pasta over high heat once you have added the egg mixture, or the sauce risks being scrambled by the heat.

Pasta with chicken, mushroom and tarragon

375 g (13 oz) fusilli, or other pasta
    shapes such as ruote, conchiglie or
    penne
2 tablespoons virgin olive oil
350 g (12 oz) chicken tenderloins, cut
    into 2 cm (3/4 inch) pieces
20 g (3/4 oz) butter
400 g (14 oz) Swiss brown or button
    mushrooms, sliced
2 garlic cloves, finely chopped
125 ml (1/2 cup) dry white wine
185 ml (3/4 cup) cream
1 teaspoon finely grated lemon zest
2 tablespoons lemon juice
1 tablespoon chopped tarragon
2 tablespoons chopped parsley
25 g (1/4 cup) grated Parmesan
    cheese, plus extra, to serve

Cook the pasta in a large saucepan of boiling salted water until *al dente*.

Meanwhile, heat 1 tablespoon of the oil in a large frying pan, add the chicken and cook over high heat for 3–4 minutes, or until lightly browned. Remove from the pan.

Heat the butter and the remaining oil, add the mushrooms and cook, stirring, over high heat for 3 minutes. Add the garlic and cook for a further 2 minutes.

Pour in the wine, then reduce the heat to low and simmer for 5 minutes, or until nearly evaporated. Add the cream and chicken and simmer for about 5 minutes, or until thickened.

Stir the lemon zest, lemon juice, tarragon, parsley and Parmesan into the sauce. Season with salt and pepper, then add the hot pasta, tossing until well combined. Serve with the extra Parmesan.

Serves 4

Pasta primavera

120 g (4 oz) broad beans, fresh or
   frozen
150 g (5½ oz) asparagus, cut into
   short lengths
350 g (12 oz) fresh tagliatelle
100 g (3½ oz) green beans, cut into
   short lengths
120 g (¾ cup) peas, fresh or frozen
30 g (1 oz) butter
1 small fennel bulb, thinly sliced
375 ml (1½ cups) thick (double/heavy)
   cream
2 tablespoons grated Parmesan
   cheese, plus extra, to serve

Bring a large saucepan of water to
the boil. Add 1 teaspoon of salt, the
broad beans and asparagus and
simmer for 3 minutes.

Remove the vegetables with a slotted
spoon and set them aside. Add the
tagliatelle to the saucepan and, when
it has softened, stir in the beans and
the peas (if you're using frozen peas,
add them a few minutes later). Cook
for about 4 minutes, or until the pasta
is *al dente*.

Meanwhile, heat the butter in a large
frying pan. Add the fennel and cook
over moderately low heat without
colouring for 5 minutes. Add the
cream, season with salt and pepper
and cook at a low simmer.

Peel the skins from the broad beans.
Drain the pasta, green beans and
peas and add them to the frying pan.
Add 2 tablespoons of Parmesan and
the broad beans and asparagus. Toss
lightly to coat. Serve immediately with
extra Parmesan.

Serves 4

Penne with veal ragout

2 onions, sliced
2 bay leaves, crushed
1.5 kg (3 lb 5 oz) veal shin, cut into
 osso buco pieces (about 4 cm/
 1½ inch thick)
250 ml (1 cup) red wine
2 x 400 g (14 oz) cans crushed
 tomatoes
375 ml (1½ cups) beef stock
2 teaspoons chopped rosemary
400 g (14 oz) penne
150 g (1 cup) frozen peas

Preheat the oven to 220°C (425°F/
Gas 7). Scatter the onion over the
bottom of a large roasting tin, lightly
spray with oil and put the bay leaves
and veal pieces on top. Season
with salt and pepper. Roast for
10–15 minutes, or until the veal is
browned. Watch the onion to make
sure that it doesn't burn.

Pour the wine over the veal and
return to the oven for a further
5 minutes. Reduce the oven to 180°C
(350°F/Gas 4), remove the tin from
the oven and pour on the tomato,
stock and 1 teaspoon of the
rosemary. Cover with foil and return to
the oven. Cook for 2 hours, or until
the veal is starting to fall from the
bone. Remove the foil and cook for a
further 15 minutes, or until the meat
loosens away from the bone and the
liquid has evaporated slightly.

Cook the pasta in a large saucepan of
boiling salted water until *al dente*.
Meanwhile, remove the veal from the
oven and cool slightly. Add the peas
and remaining rosemary, place over a
hotplate and cook over medium heat
for 5 minutes, or until the peas are
cooked. Drain the pasta, divide among
four bowls and top with the ragout.

Serves 4

Pasta with lentils, winter vegetables and thyme

1 litre (4 cups) chicken stock
500 g (1 lb 2 oz) conchigliette (small
   shell pasta) or orecchiette
2 tablespoons olive oil
1 onion, chopped
2 carrots, diced
3 celery stalks, diced
3 garlic cloves, finely chopped
1½ tablespoons chopped thyme
400 g (14 oz) cooked green lentils, or
   canned
virgin olive oil, to drizzle
grated Parmesan cheese, to serve
   (optional)

Boil the chicken stock in a large saucepan for 10 minutes, or until reduced to 500 ml (2 cups) of liquid. Meanwhile, cook the pasta in a saucepan of boiling salted water until *al dente*.

Heat the oil in a large deep frying pan. Add the onion, carrot and celery and cook over medium heat for 10 minutes, or until browned. Add 2 cloves of the garlic and 1 tablespoon of the thyme and cook for a further minute. Pour in the stock, bring to the boil and cook for 8 minutes, or until reduced slightly and the vegetables are tender. Gently stir in the lentils until heated through.

Stir in the remaining garlic and thyme, and season with plenty of salt and freshly ground black pepper — the stock should be slightly syrupy at this point. Combine the hot pasta with the lentil sauce in a large bowl, drizzle generously with the virgin olive oil and serve with Parmesan, if desired.

Serves 4

Penne with meatballs and tomato

Meatballs
2 slices white bread, crusts removed
60 ml (¼ cup) milk
500 g (1 lb 2 oz) minced (ground)
   pork and veal (see Note)
1 small onion, finely chopped
2 garlic cloves, finely chopped
3 tablespoons finely chopped flat-leaf
   (Italian) parsley
2 teaspoons finely grated lemon zest
1 egg, lightly beaten
50 g (½ cup) grated Parmesan
   cheese
plain (all-purpose) flour, to coat
2 tablespoons olive oil

125 ml (½ cup) white wine
2 x 400 g (14 oz) cans chopped
   tomatoes
1 tablespoon tomato paste (purée)
1 teaspoon caster (superfine) sugar
½ teaspoon dried oregano
500 g (1 lb 2 oz) penne rigate (penne
   with ridges)
oregano leaves, to garnish

To make the meatballs, soak the bread in the milk for 5 minutes, then squeeze out any moisture. Put the bread, mince, onion, garlic, parsley, zest, egg and Parmesan in a bowl, season and mix well with your hands.

Shape into walnut-size balls using damp hands, and roll lightly in the flour. Heat the oil in a large deep frying pan and cook the meatballs in batches over medium heat, turning frequently, for 10 minutes, or until brown all over. Remove with a slotted spoon and drain on paper towels.

Pour the wine into the same frying pan and boil over medium heat for 2–3 minutes, or until it evaporates a little. Add the tomato, tomato paste, sugar and dried oregano. Reduce the heat, then simmer for 20 minutes to thicken the sauce. Add the meatballs and simmer for 10 minutes. Meanwhile, cook the pasta in a saucepan of boiling salted water until *al dente*.

To serve, divide the hot pasta among six serving plates and spoon some meatballs and sauce over the top of each. Garnish with the oregano.

Serves 6

Note: Use minced beef instead of the pork and veal, if you prefer.

Spaghetti with anchovies, capers and chilli

400 g (14 oz) spaghettini (thin
  spaghetti)
125 ml (½ cup) olive oil
4 garlic cloves, finely chopped
10 anchovy fillets, chopped
1 tablespoon baby capers, rinsed and
  squeezed dry
1 teaspoon chilli flakes
2 tablespoons lemon juice
2 teaspoons finely grated lemon zest
3 tablespoons chopped parsley
3 tablespoons chopped basil leaves
3 tablespoons chopped mint
50 g (½ cup) coarsely grated
  Parmesan cheese, plus extra,
  to serve
extra virgin olive oil, to drizzle

Cook the pasta in a saucepan of
boiling salted water until *al dente*.

Heat the oil in a frying pan and cook
the garlic over medium heat for
2–3 minutes, or until starting to
brown. Add the anchovies, capers
and chilli and cook for 1 minute.

Add the hot pasta to the pan with the
lemon juice, zest, parsley, basil, mint
and Parmesan. Season with salt and
pepper and toss together well.

To serve, drizzle with a little extra oil
and sprinkle with Parmesan.

Serves 4

Blue cheese and walnut lasagnette

375 g (13 oz) lasagnette
100 g (1 cup) walnuts
40 g (1½ oz) butter
3 French shallots, finely chopped
1 tablespoon brandy or cognac
250 ml (1 cup) crème fraîche
200 g (7 oz) gorgonzola cheese,
    crumbled (see Note)
70 g (2½ oz) baby English spinach
    leaves

Preheat the oven to 200°C (400°F/ Gas 6). Cook the pasta in a large saucepan of boiling salted water until *al dente*. Drain, return to the pan and keep warm.

Meanwhile, place the walnuts on a baking tray and roast for 5 minutes, or until golden and toasted. Cool, then roughly chop.

Heat the butter in a large saucepan, add the shallots and cook over medium heat for 1–2 minutes, or until soft, taking care not to brown. Add the brandy and simmer for 1 minute, then stir in the crème fraîche and gorgonzola. Cook for 3–4 minutes, or until the cheese has melted and the sauce has thickened.

Stir in the spinach and toasted walnuts, reserving 1 tablespoon for garnish. Heat gently until the spinach has just wilted. Season with salt and cracked black pepper. Gently mix the sauce through the pasta. Divide among serving plates and sprinkle with the reserved walnuts.

Serves 4

Note: The gorgonzola needs to be young as this gives a sweeter, milder flavour to the sauce.

Pasta with grilled capsicum

6 large red capsicums (peppers),
  halved
400 g (14 oz) pasta gnocchi (see
  Note)
2 tablespoons olive oil
1 onion, thinly sliced
3 garlic cloves, finely chopped
2 tablespoons shredded basil leaves
whole basil leaves, to garnish
shaved Parmesan cheese, to serve

Cut the capsicums into large flattish
pieces. Cook, skin side up, under a
hot grill (broiler) until the skin blackens
and blisters. Place in a plastic bag
and leave to cool, then peel the skin.

Cook the pasta in a saucepan of
boiling salted water until *al dente*.
Meanwhile, heat the oil in a large
frying pan, add the onion and garlic
and cook over medium heat for
5 minutes, or until soft. Cut one
capsicum into thin strips and add to
the onion mixture.

Chop the remaining capsicum, then
purée in a food processor until
smooth. Add to the onion mixture and
cook over low heat for 5 minutes, or
until warmed through.

Toss the sauce through the hot pasta.
Season, then stir in the shredded
basil. Garnish with the basil leaves
and serve with the Parmesan.

Serves 4–6

Note: Not to be confused with the
potato dumplings of the same name,
pasta gnocchi is, as the name
suggests, similar in shape to potato
gnocchi. If unavailable, use conchiglie
or orecchiette.

Spaghetti vongole

1 kg (2 lb 4 oz) baby clams (vongole)
375 g (13 oz) spaghetti
125 ml (1/2 cup) virgin olive oil
40 g (1 1/2 oz) butter
1 small onion, very finely chopped
6 large garlic cloves, finely chopped
125 ml (1/2 cup) dry white wine
1 small red chilli, seeded and finely
  chopped
15 g (1/2 cup) chopped flat-leaf (Italian)
  parsley

Scrub the clams with a small stiff brush to remove any grit, discarding any that are open or cracked. Then soak and rinse the clams in several changes of water over an hour or so until the water is clean and free of grit. Drain and set aside.

Cook the pasta in a saucepan of boiling salted water until *al dente*.

Heat the oil and 1 tablespoon of the butter in a large saucepan over medium heat. Add the onion and half the garlic and cook for 10 minutes, or until lightly golden — ensure the garlic doesn't start to burn. Add the wine and cook for 2 minutes. Then add the clams, chilli and the remaining butter and garlic and cook, covered, for 8 minutes, shaking regularly, until the clams pop open — discard any that are still closed.

Stir in the parsley and season. Add the hot pasta and toss well.

Serves 4

Penne all'arrabbiata

2 tablespoons olive oil
2 large garlic cloves, thinly sliced
1–2 medium-sized dried chillies
2 x 400 g (14 oz) cans tomatoes
400 g (14 oz) penne or rigatoni
1 basil sprig, torn into pieces

Heat the olive oil in a saucepan and add the garlic and chillies. Cook over low heat until the garlic is light golden brown. Turn the chillies over during cooking so both sides get a chance to infuse in the oil and turn slightly nutty in flavour. Add the tomatoes and season with salt. Cook gently, breaking up the tomatoes with a wooden spoon, for 20–30 minutes, or until the sauce is rich and thick.

Meanwhile, cook the pasta in a large saucepan of boiling salted water until *al dente*. Drain.

Add the basil to the sauce and season just before serving, tossed with the pasta. If you prefer a hotter sauce, break open the chilli to release the seeds.

Serves 4

Pasta alla Norma

185 ml (³/₄ cup) olive oil
1 onion, finely chopped
2 garlic cloves, finely chopped
2 x 400 g (14 oz) cans chopped
  tomatoes
400 g (14 oz) bucatini or spaghetti
1 large eggplant (aubergine), about
  500 g (1 lb 2 oz)
30 g (½ cup) basil leaves, torn, plus
  extra, to garnish
60 g (½ cup) ricotta salata (see Note),
  crumbled
45 g (½ cup) grated pecorino or
  Parmesan cheese
1 tablespoon extra virgin olive oil, to
  drizzle

Heat 2 tablespoons of the oil in a frying pan and cook the onion over medium heat for 5 minutes, or until softened. Stir in the garlic and cook for 30 seconds. Add the tomato and season. Reduce the heat to low and cook for 20–25 minutes, or until the sauce has thickened and reduced.

Cook the pasta in a saucepan of boiling salted water until *al dente*. Meanwhile, cut the eggplant lengthways into 5 mm (¼ inch) thick slices. Heat the remaining olive oil in a large frying pan. When the oil is hot but not smoking, add the eggplant slices a few at a time and cook for 3–5 minutes, or until lightly browned on both sides. Remove from the pan and drain on crumpled paper towels.

Add the eggplant to the sauce with the basil, stirring over very low heat.

Add the hot pasta to the sauce with half each of the ricotta and pecorino and toss together well. Serve immediately, sprinkled with the remaining cheeses and extra basil and drizzled with oil.

Serves 4–6

Note: Ricotta salata is a lightly salted, pressed ricotta cheese. If unavailable, use a mild feta cheese.

Spaghetti marinara

500 g (1 lb 2 oz) spaghetti
1 tablespoon olive oil
1 onion, finely chopped
3 garlic cloves, finely chopped
2 x 400 g (14 oz) cans chopped
   tomatoes
2 tablespoons tomato paste (purée)
170 ml (2/3 cup) dry white wine
2 teaspoons soft brown sugar
1 teaspoon finely grated lemon zest
2 tablespoons torn basil leaves, plus
   extra, to garnish
2 tablespoons finely chopped flat-leaf
   (Italian) parsley
12 medium raw prawns (shrimp),
   peeled and deveined, with tails intact
8 black mussels, scrubbed and
   beards removed
8 large white scallops, without roe
2 small squid tubes, cleaned and cut
   into 1 cm (1/2 inch) rings

Cook the pasta in a saucepan of boiling salted water until *al dente*.

Meanwhile, heat the oil in a large saucepan, add the onion and cook over medium heat for 5–8 minutes, or until golden. Add the garlic, tomato, tomato paste, wine, sugar, lemon zest, 1 tablespoon of the basil, parsley and 250 ml (1 cup) water. Cook, stirring occasionally, for 1 hour, or until the sauce is reduced and thickened. Season.

Add the prawns and mussels and cook for 1 minute, then add the scallops and cook for 2 minutes. Stir in the squid and cook for 1 minute more, or until all the seafood is cooked through and tender.

Add the hot pasta to the sauce with the remaining basil and toss together until well combined. Serve.

Serves 4

Pasta with lamb shank, rosemary and red wine ragù

1½ tablespoons olive oil
1 large onion, finely chopped
1 large carrot, finely diced
2 celery stalks, finely diced
2 bay leaves
1.5 kg (3 lb 5 oz) lamb shanks, trimmed of excess fat
4 garlic cloves, finely chopped
1 tablespoon finely chopped rosemary
750 ml (3 cups) dry red wine
1 litre (4 cups) beef stock
500 ml (2 cups) tomato passata
½ teaspoon finely grated lemon zest
500 g (1 lb 2 oz) pappardelle or any ribbon-shaped pasta
flat-leaf (Italian) parsley leaves, to garnish

Heat 1 tablespoon of the oil in a large, deep saucepan. Add the onion, carrot, celery and bay leaves and cook over medium heat, stirring often, for about 10 minutes, or until the onion is lightly browned. Remove from the pan. Heat a little more oil in the pan and cook the shanks in two batches, turning occasionally, for 15 minutes, or until browned. Remove from the pan.

Add the garlic and rosemary to the pan and cook for 30 seconds, or until lightly golden and fragrant. Return the vegetables to the pan, then stir in the wine, stock, passata, zest and 250 ml (1 cup) water. Using a wooden spoon, scrape up any sediment stuck to the base of the pan. Add the shanks and bring to the boil — removing any scum that rises to the surface. Reduce the heat and simmer, uncovered, for 2¼ hours, or until the lamb is very tender and the sauce is thick and glossy. Meanwhile, cook the pasta in a saucepan of boiling salted water until *al dente*.

Remove the shanks from the sauce and remove the meat from the bones using a fork and tongs. Return the meat to the sauce and stir to heat through. Season. Toss the hot pasta through the sauce. Serve with parsley.

Serves 6–8

Linguine with ham, artichoke and lemon sauce

500 g (1 lb 2 oz) fresh linguine
25 g (1 oz) butter
2 large garlic cloves, chopped
150 g (5½ oz) marinated artichokes, drained and quartered
150 g (5½ oz) sliced leg ham, cut into strips
300 ml (10½ fl oz) cream
2 teaspoons coarsely grated lemon zest
15 g (½ cup) basil, torn
35 g (⅓ cup) grated Parmesan cheese

Cook the pasta in a large saucepan of boiling salted water until *al dente*. Drain, then return to the pan.

Meanwhile, melt the butter in a large frying pan, add the garlic and cook over medium heat for 1 minute, or until fragrant. Add the artichokes and ham and cook for a further 2 minutes.

Add the cream and zest, reduce the heat and simmer for 5 minutes, gently breaking up the artichokes with a wooden spoon.

Pour the sauce over the pasta, then add the basil and Parmesan and toss well until the pasta is evenly coated. Divide among four serving plates and serve immediately.

Serves 4

Buckwheat pasta with cabbage, potato and cheese sauce

350 g (12 oz) savoy cabbage, roughly
  chopped
175 g (6 oz) potatoes, cut into 2 cm
  (³/₄ inch) cubes
500 g (1 lb 2 oz) buckwheat pasta
  (pizzoccheri)
4 tablespoons extra virgin olive oil
1 small bunch sage, finely chopped
2 garlic cloves, finely chopped
350 g (12 oz) mixed cheeses (such as
  mascarpone, fontina, Taleggio and
  Gorgonzola)
grated Parmesan cheese, to serve

Bring a large saucepan of salted water to the boil. Add the cabbage, potato and the pasta and cook for 3–5 minutes, or until the pasta and vegetables are cooked through. Drain, reserving about a cup of the cooking water.

Dry the saucepan, then add the olive oil and gently cook the sage and garlic for 1 minute. Add the mixed cheeses to the pan. Mix briefly, and add the pasta, cabbage and potatoes. Season with salt and pepper.

Remove the saucepan from the heat and gently stir the mixture together, adding some of the reserved pasta water to loosen it up a little if necessary. Serve with Parmesan sprinkled over the top.

Serves 6

Note: Buckwheat pasta is called *pizzoccheri* in Italy. This type of pasta is popular in Valtellina, near the Swiss border, and is traditionally served with potatoes, cabbage and cheese.

Ravioli with prawns and creamy lime sauce

50 g (1³/₄ oz) butter
4 garlic cloves, crushed
750 g (1 lb 10 oz) medium raw
    prawns (shrimp), peeled and
    deveined
1½ tablespoons plain (all-purpose)
    flour
375 ml (1½ cups) fish stock
500 ml (2 cups) cream
5 makrut (kaffir) lime leaves, shredded
650 g (1 lb 7 oz) seafood ravioli (see
    Note)
3 teaspoons fish sauce

Melt the butter in a large deep frying pan and cook the garlic over medium heat for 1 minute. Add the prawns and cook for 3–4 minutes, or until they turn pink and are cooked through. Remove from the pan, leaving any juices in the pan. Add the flour and stir for 1 minute, or until lightly golden. Gradually stir in the stock, then add the cream and lime leaves. Reduce the heat and simmer for 10 minutes, or until slightly thickened.

Meanwhile, cook the pasta in a large saucepan of boiling salted water until *al dente*. Drain.

Stir the fish sauce through the cream sauce, add the prawns and stir until warmed through. Divide the pasta among four warm serving plates and spoon on the prawns and sauce. Season with salt and cracked black pepper and serve.

Serves 4

Note: Seafood ravioli is available from speciality pasta shops, but if it is unavailable you can use ricotta ravioli instead — the flavours work well.

Pasta with pumpkin and feta

1 kg (2 lb 4 oz) butternut pumpkin
  (squash), peeled and cut into 2 cm
  ($^3/_4$ inch) chunks
1 red onion, thinly sliced
8 garlic cloves, unpeeled
1 tablespoon rosemary leaves
80 ml ($^1/_3$ cup) olive oil
400 g (14 oz) casserechi pasta, or
  macaroni, gemelli or other short
  pasta
200 g (7 oz) marinated feta cheese,
  crumbled
2 tablespoons grated Parmesan
  cheese
2 tablespoons finely chopped parsley

Preheat the oven to 200°C (400°F/
Gas 6). Put the pumpkin, onion, garlic
and rosemary in a roasting tin, then
drizzle with 1 tablespoon of the oil.
Season. Using your hands, rub the
oil over all the ingredients until well
coated. Roast for 30 minutes, or
until the pumpkin is soft and starting
to caramelize.

Cook the pasta in a saucepan of
boiling salted water until al dente.

Squeeze the roasted garlic out of its
skin and place it in a bowl with the
remaining oil. Mash with a fork.

Add the garlic oil to the hot pasta,
then the remaining ingredients. Toss
well and season.

Serves 4

Ham tortellini with nutty herb sauce

500 g (1 lb 2 oz) ham and cheese
  tortellini
60 g (2¼ oz) butter
100 g (1 cup) walnuts, chopped
100 g (⅔ cup) pine nuts
2 tablespoons finely chopped flat-leaf
  (Italian) parsley
2 teaspoons chopped thyme
60 g (¼ cup) ricotta cheese
60 ml (¼ cup) thick (double/heavy)
  cream

Cook the pasta in a large saucepan of boiling water until *al dente*. Drain and return to the pan.

Meanwhile, heat the butter in a frying pan over medium heat until foaming. Add the walnuts and pine nuts and stir for 5 minutes, or until golden brown. Add the parsley and thyme and season to taste.

Beat the ricotta and cream together. Add the nutty sauce to the pasta and toss. Divide among serving bowls and top with the ricotta cream.

Serves 4–6

Tagliatelle with prawns and leek in saffron cream

40 g (1½ oz) butter
1 small leek, julienned
4 garlic cloves, finely chopped
pinch of saffron threads
125 ml (½ cup) dry vermouth
250 ml (1 cup) fish stock
300 ml (10½ fl oz) thick
  (double/heavy) cream
400 g (14 oz) fresh tagliatelle or any
  long, flat pasta
24 medium raw prawns (shrimp),
  peeled and deveined, with tails
  intact
1 tablespoon lemon juice
1 tablespoon finely chopped chervil,
  plus extra, to garnish (see Variation)

Melt the butter in a saucepan over medium heat, add the leek and garlic and cook for 5 minutes, or until the leek is soft and translucent. Add the saffron, vermouth and fish stock and bring to the boil, skimming off any scum that rises to the surface. Reduce the heat to low and simmer for 10 minutes, or until the sauce has reduced by half. Pour in the cream and simmer for 15 minutes, or until the sauce has thickened and reduced by about a third.

Meanwhile, cook the pasta in a saucepan of boiling salted water until *al dente*.

Add the prawns to the sauce and simmer for 2–3 minutes, or until cooked through. Remove from the heat and stir in the lemon juice and chervil. Season well, then toss through the hot pasta. Serve immediately, garnished with a little extra chervil, if desired.

Serves 4–6

Note: This creamy pasta is very rich and more suitable as a starter than a main course.
Variation: Parsley or dill can be used in place of chervil.

Orecchiette with cauliflower, bacon and pecorino

750 g (1 lb 10 oz) cauliflower, cut into florets
500 g (1 lb 2 oz) orecchiette (see Note)
125 ml (1/2 cup) olive oil, plus extra, to drizzle
150 g (5 1/2 oz) bacon, diced
2 garlic cloves, finely chopped
80 g (1/2 cup) pine nuts, toasted
45 g (1/2 cup) grated pecorino cheese
15 g (1/2 cup) chopped flat-leaf (Italian) parsley
60 g (3/4 cup) fresh breadcrumbs, toasted

Bring a large saucepan of boiling salted water to the boil and cook the cauliflower for 5–6 minutes, or until tender. Drain.

Cook the pasta in a large saucepan of boiling salted water until *al dente*.

Heat the oil in a frying pan and cook the bacon over medium heat for 4–5 minutes, or until just crisp. Add the garlic and cook for 1 minute, or until just beginning to turn golden. Add the cauliflower and toss well.

Add the cooked pasta to the pan with the pine nuts, pecorino cheese, parsley and 40 g (1/2 cup) of the breadcrumbs and mix. Season, sprinkle with the remaining breadcrumbs and drizzle with a little extra oil.

Serves 4

Note: Orecchiette means 'little ears' in Italian, and the name of the pasta is a literal description of the shape — although some brands look more like curls than ears. If unavailable, use conchiglie or cavatelli.

Pasta amatriciana

2 tablespoons olive oil
200 g (7 oz) pancetta, thinly sliced
1 red onion, finely chopped
2 garlic cloves, finely chopped
1 teaspoon chilli flakes
2 teaspoons finely chopped rosemary
2 x 400 g (14 oz) cans chopped
  tomatoes
500 g (1 lb 2 oz) bucatini or spaghetti
15 g (½ cup) chopped flat-leaf (Italian)
  parsley

Heat the oil in a frying pan and cook the pancetta over medium heat for 6–8 minutes, or until crisp. Add the onion, garlic, chilli flakes and chopped rosemary and cook for 4–5 minutes more, or until the onion has softened.

Add the tomato to the pan, season with salt and pepper, and bring to the boil. Reduce the heat to low and simmer for 20 minutes, or until the sauce is reduced and very thick.

Meanwhile, cook the pasta in a large saucepan of boiling salted water until al dente.

Toss the sauce with the hot pasta and parsley, then serve.

Serves 4

Veal tortellini with baked pumpkin and basil butter

1 kg (2 lb 4 oz) jap pumpkin, cut into
  2 cm (³/₄ inch) cubes
600 g (1 lb 5 oz) veal tortellini
100 g (3½ oz) butter
3 garlic cloves, crushed
80 g (½ cup) pine nuts
45 g (³/₄ cup) firmly packed shredded
  basil
200 g (7 oz) feta cheese, crumbled

Preheat the oven to 220°C (425°F/ Gas 7). Line a baking tray with baking paper. Place the pumpkin on the prepared tray and season well with salt and cracked black pepper. Bake for 30 minutes, or until tender.

Meanwhile, cook the pasta in a large saucepan of boiling salted water until *al dente*. Drain and return to the pan.

Heat the butter over medium heat in a small frying pan until foaming. Add the garlic and pine nuts and cook for 3–5 minutes, or until the nuts are starting to turn golden. Remove from the heat and add the basil. Toss the basil butter, pumpkin and feta through the cooked pasta and serve.

Serves 4

Pasta with roast chicken, pine nuts and lemon

1.3 kg (3 lb) chicken
1 garlic bulb, cloves separated and
  left unpeeled
60 ml ($\frac{1}{4}$ cup) olive oil
30 g (1 oz) butter, softened
1 tablespoon finely chopped thyme
125 ml ($\frac{1}{2}$ cup) lemon juice
500 g (1 lb 2 oz) bavette or spaghetti
2 tablespoons currants
1 teaspoon finely grated lemon zest
50 g ($\frac{1}{3}$ cup) pine nuts, toasted
15 g ($\frac{1}{2}$ cup) finely chopped flat-leaf
  (Italian) parsley

Preheat the oven to 200°C (400°F/ Gas 6). Remove the neck from the inside of the chicken and place the neck in a roasting tin. Rinse the inside of the chicken with cold water and shake out any excess. Insert the garlic cloves into the cavity, then put the chicken in the roasting tin.

Combine the oil, butter, thyme and lemon juice, then rub over the chicken. Season the chicken. Roast for 1 hour, or until the skin is golden and the juices run clear when the thigh is pierced with a skewer. Transfer the chicken to a bowl to catch any juices while resting. Remove the garlic from the cavity, cool, then squeeze the garlic cloves out of their skins and finely chop.

Cook the pasta in a large pan of boiling salted water until *al dente*. Meanwhile, pour the juices from the roasting tin into a saucepan and discard the neck. Add the currants, zest and chopped garlic, then simmer over low heat. Remove all the meat from the chicken and shred into bite-size pieces. Add the resting juices to the pan.

Add the chicken meat, pine nuts, parsley and the sauce to the hot pasta and toss well. Season with salt and pepper and serve.

Serves 4–6

Pasta boscaiola

30 g (1 oz) butter
4 rashers bacon, diced
2 garlic cloves, finely chopped
300 g (10½ oz) Swiss brown or
  button mushrooms, sliced
60 ml (¼ cup) dry white wine
375 ml (1½ cups) cream
1 teaspoon chopped thyme
500 g (1 lb 2 oz) veal tortellini
50 g (½ cup) grated Parmesan
  cheese
1 tablespoon chopped flat-leaf
  (Italian) parsley

Melt the butter in a large frying pan, add the bacon and cook over medium heat for 5 minutes, or until crisp. Add the garlic and cook for 2 minutes, then add the mushrooms, cooking for a further 8 minutes, or until softened.

Stir in the wine and cream and add the thyme and bring to the boil. Reduce the heat to low and simmer for 10 minutes, or until the sauce has thickened. Meanwhile, cook the pasta in a large saucepan of boiling salted water until *al dente*

Combine the sauce with the hot pasta, Parmesan and parsley. Season to taste and serve immediately.

Serves 4–6

Spaghettini with squid in black ink

1 kg (2 lb 4 oz) medium squid
2 tablespoons olive oil
1 onion, finely chopped
6 garlic cloves, finely chopped
1 bay leaf
1 small red chilli, seeded and thinly
  sliced
80 ml (⅓ cup) white wine
80 ml (⅓ cup) dry vermouth
250 ml (1 cup) fish stock
60 g (¼ cup) tomato paste (purée)
500 ml (2 cups) tomato passata
15 g (½ oz) squid ink
500 g (1 lb 2 oz) spaghettini
½ teaspoon Pernod (optional)
4 tablespoons chopped flat-leaf
  (Italian) parsley
1 garlic clove, extra, crushed

To clean the squid, pull the tentacles away from the hood (the intestines should come away at the same time). Remove the intestines by cutting under the eyes, and remove the beak by using your fingers to push up the centre. Pull out the transparent quill from inside the body. Remove any white membrane. Cut the squid into thin slices.

Heat the oil in a saucepan over medium heat. Add the onion and cook until lightly golden. Add the garlic, bay leaf and chilli and cook for 2 minutes, or until the garlic is lightly golden. Stir in the wine, vermouth, stock, tomato paste, passata and 250 ml (1 cup) water, then increase the heat to high and bring to the boil. Reduce to a simmer and cook for 45 minutes, or until the liquid has reduced by half. Add the squid ink and cook for 2 minutes, or until the sauce is evenly black and glossy. Meanwhile, cook the pasta in a large saucepan of boiling salted water until *al dente*.

Add the squid rings and Pernod, stir well, then cook for 4–5 minutes, or until they turn opaque and are cooked through. Stir in the parsley and the extra garlic and season. Toss through the hot pasta and serve immediately.

Serves 4–6

Gnocchi with gorgonzola cream

500 g (1 lb 2 oz) ready-made potato
  gnocchi
walnuts, to garnish
375 ml (1½ cups) cream
200 g (7 oz) mild gorgonzola cheese,
  crumbled
2 tablespoons grated Parmesan
  cheese
40 g (1½ oz) butter
pinch of grated nutmeg

Cook the gnocchi in a large saucepan of boiling salted water until *al dente*.

Spread the walnuts on a baking tray and toast in a 180°C (350°F/Gas 4) oven for 5–8 minutes, or until lightly coloured. Alternatively, place them on a tray under a hot grill (broiler). Once they start to brown, nuts burn very quickly, so watch them carefully. Cool, then roughly chop.

Put the cream, gorgonzola, Parmesan and butter in a saucepan and heat over low heat, stirring occasionally, for 3 minutes, or until the cheeses have melted into a smooth sauce.

Stir in the nutmeg and serve immediately over the hot pasta. Garnish with the walnuts.

Serves 4–6

Note: This dish is very rich and is recommended as a starter rather than a main course.

Tagliatelle with walnut sauce

200 g (2 cups) shelled walnuts
20 g (1/3 cup) roughly chopped parsley
50 g (1 3/4 oz) butter
200 ml (7 fl oz) extra virgin olive oil
1 garlic clove, crushed
30 g (1 oz) Parmesan cheese, grated
100 ml (3 1/2 fl oz) thick (double/heavy) cream
400 g (14 oz) pasta, such as tagliatelle

Lightly toast the walnuts in a dry frying pan over moderately high heat for 2 minutes, or until browned. Set aside to cool for 5 minutes.

Put the walnuts in a food processor with the parsley and blend until finely chopped. Add the butter and mix together. Gradually pour in the olive oil in a steady stream with the motor running. Add the garlic, Parmesan and cream. Season with salt and black pepper.

Cook the pasta in a large saucepan of boiling salted water until *al dente*. Drain, then toss through the sauce to serve.

Serves 4

Pasta bolognese

2 tablespoons olive oil
2 garlic cloves, finely chopped
1 large onion, finely chopped
1 carrot, finely chopped
1 celery stalk, finely chopped
50 g (1³/₄ oz) pancetta or bacon,
  finely chopped
500 g (1 lb 2 oz) minced (ground) beef
500 ml (2 cups) beef stock
375 ml (1¹/₂ cups) red wine
2 x 400 g (14 oz) cans chopped
  tomatoes
2 tablespoons tomato paste (purée)
1 teaspoon sugar
500 g (1 lb 2 oz) fresh tagliatelle (see
  Note)
shaved Parmesan cheese, to serve

Heat the oil in a large deep saucepan.
Add the garlic, onion, carrot, celery
and pancetta and cook, stirring, over
medium heat for about 5 minutes, or
until softened.

Add the mince and break up any
lumps with the back of a spoon,
stirring until just browned. Add the
stock, red wine, tomatoes, tomato
paste and sugar. Bring to the boil,
then reduce the heat to very low and
simmer, covered, stirring occasionally,
for 1¹/₂ hours. Remove the lid and
simmer, stirring occasionally, for a
further 1¹/₂ hours. Season to taste
with salt and freshly ground pepper.
While the meat is cooking, cook the
pasta in a saucepan of boiling salted
water until *al dente*.

To serve, spoon the sauce over the
hot pasta and sprinkle with some of
the shaved Parmesan.

Serves 4–6

Note: Traditionally, bolognese was
served with tagliatelle, but now we
tend to serve it with spaghetti.

Spaghetti puttanesca

6 large ripe tomatoes
375 g (13 oz) spaghetti
80 ml (1/3 cup) olive oil
2 onions, finely chopped
3 garlic cloves, finely chopped
1/2 teaspoon chilli flakes
4 tablespoons capers, rinsed and
  squeezed dry
7–8 anchovies in oil, drained and
  chopped
150 g (5 1/2 oz) Kalamata olives
3 tablespoons chopped flat-leaf
  (Italian) parsley

Score a cross in the base of each tomato. Put the tomatoes in a bowl of boiling water for 30 seconds, then plunge into cold water and peel the skin away from the cross. Dice the tomato flesh. Cook the pasta in a large saucepan of boiling salted water until *al dente*.

Heat the oil in a saucepan, add the onion and cook over medium heat for 5 minutes. Add the garlic and chilli flakes and cook for 30 seconds before adding the capers, anchovies and diced tomato. Simmer over low heat for 5–10 minutes, or until thick and pulpy. Stir in the olives and parsley.

Add the hot pasta to the sauce and toss through until well combined. Season with salt and freshly ground black pepper and serve.

Serves 4

Pasta with artichokes and grilled chicken

1 tablespoon olive oil
3 chicken breast fillets
500 g (1 lb 2 oz) pasta, such as
  tagliatelle or any long, flat pasta
8 slices prosciutto
280 g (10 oz) jar artichokes in oil,
  drained and quartered, oil reserved
150 g (5½ oz) semi-dried (sun-blushed)
  tomatoes, thinly sliced
90 g (3¼ oz) baby rocket (arugula)
  leaves
2–3 tablespoons balsamic vinegar

Lightly brush a chargrill pan (griddle) or frying pan with oil and heat over high heat. Cook the chicken fillets for 6–8 minutes each side, or until they are cooked through. Thinly slice and set aside.

Cook the pasta in a large saucepan of boiling salted water until *al dente*. Drain the pasta and return to the pan to keep warm. Meanwhile, place the prosciutto under a hot grill (broiler) and grill (broil) for 2 minutes each side, or until crisp. Cool slightly and break into pieces.

Combine the pasta with the chicken, prosciutto, artichokes, tomato and rocket in a bowl and toss. Whisk together 60 ml (¼ cup) of the reserved artichoke oil and the balsamic vinegar and toss through the pasta mixture. Season and serve.

Serves 6

Pasta with creamy tomato and bacon sauce

400 g (14 oz) curly pasta such as cresti di gallo, cotelli or fusilli (see Notes)
1 tablespoon olive oil
175 g (6 oz) streaky bacon, thinly sliced (see Notes)
500 g (1 lb 2 oz) Roma (plum) tomatoes, roughly chopped
125 ml (1/2 cup) thick (double/heavy) cream
2 tablespoons sun-dried tomato pesto
2 tablespoons finely chopped flat-leaf (Italian) parsley
50 g (1/2 cup) finely grated Parmesan cheese

Cook the pasta in a large saucepan of boiling salted water until *al dente*. Drain and return to the saucepan.

Meanwhile, heat the oil in a frying pan, add the bacon and cook over high heat for 2 minutes, or until starting to brown. Reduce the heat to medium, add the tomato and cook, stirring frequently, for 2 minutes, or until the tomato has softened but still holds its shape.

Add the cream and tomato pesto and stir until heated through. Remove from the heat, add the parsley and then toss the sauce through the pasta with the grated Parmesan.

Serves 4

Notes: Cresti di gallo pasta is named after the Italian word for 'cockscombs' because of its similarity to the crest of a rooster.
Streaky bacon is the tail fatty end of bacon rashers. It is fattier but adds to the flavour of the meal. You can use 175 g (6 oz) bacon rashers if you prefer.

Angel hair pasta with scallops, rocket and lemon

350 g (12 oz) angel hair pasta
100 g (3½ oz) butter
3 garlic cloves, finely chopped
24 scallops, without roe
150 g (5½ oz) baby rocket (arugula)
    leaves
2 teaspoons finely grated lemon zest
60 ml (¼ cup) lemon juice
125 g (4½ oz) semi-dried (sun-
    blushed) tomatoes, thinly sliced

Cook the pasta in a large saucepan of boiling salted water until *al dente*.

Melt the butter in a small saucepan, add the garlic and cook over low heat, stirring, for 1 minute. Remove the pan from the heat.

Heat a lightly greased chargrill pan (griddle) over high heat. Lightly brush both sides of the scallops with the garlic butter and season with salt and pepper. When the chargrill pan is very hot, sear the scallops for 1 minute on each side, or until golden and just cooked through. Keep warm.

Toss the hot pasta with the rocket, lemon zest and juice, tomato and the remaining garlic butter until combined. Season. Divide among four bowls and top with the scallops.

Serves 4

Note: Put the scallops on at the same time as the pasta.

Risoni risotto with mushrooms and pancetta

25 g (1 oz) butter
2 garlic cloves, finely chopped
150 g (5½ oz) piece pancetta, diced
400 g (14 oz) button mushrooms, sliced
500 g (1 lb 2 oz) risoni (rice-shaped pasta)
1 litre (4 cups) chicken stock
125 ml (½ cup) cream
50 g (½ cup) finely grated Parmesan cheese
4 tablespoons finely chopped flat-leaf (Italian) parsley

Melt the butter in a saucepan, add the garlic and cook over medium heat for 30 seconds, then increase the heat to high, add the pancetta and cook for 3–5 minutes, or until crisp. Add the mushrooms and cook for a further 3–5 minutes, or until softened.

Add the risoni, stir until it is coated in the mixture, then add the stock and bring to the boil. Reduce the heat to medium and cook, covered, for 15–20 minutes, or until nearly all the liquid has evaporated and the risoni is tender.

Stir in the cream and cook, uncovered, for 3 minutes, stirring occasionally, until the cream is absorbed. Stir in 35 g (⅓ cup) of the Parmesan and all the parsley and season with salt and cracked black pepper. Divide among four serving bowls and serve sprinkled with the remaining Parmesan.

Serves 4

Pasta gnocchi with sausage and tomato

500 g (1 lb 2 oz) pasta gnocchi (see Note)
2 tablespoons olive oil
400 g (14 oz) thin Italian sausages
1 red onion, finely chopped
2 garlic cloves, finely chopped
2 x 400 g (14 oz) cans chopped tomatoes
1 teaspoon caster (superfine) sugar
25 g (1/2 cup) firmly packed basil, torn
45 g (1/2 cup) grated pecorino cheese

Cook the pasta in a large saucepan of boiling salted water until *al dente*. Drain and return the pasta to the pan.

Heat 2 teaspoons of the oil in a large frying pan. Add the sausages and cook, turning, for 5 minutes, or until browned and cooked through. Drain on paper towels, then slice when cool enough to touch. Keep warm.

Wipe clean the frying pan and heat the remaining oil. Add the onion and garlic and cook over medium heat for 2 minutes, or until the onion has softened. Add the tomato, sugar and 250 ml (1 cup) water and season well with cracked black pepper. Reduce the heat and simmer for 12 minutes, or until thickened and reduced a little.

Pour the sauce over the cooked pasta and stir through the sausage, then the basil and half of the cheese. Divide among serving plates and serve hot with the remaining cheese sprinkled over the top.

Serves 4–6

Note: Not to be confused with the potato dumplings of the same name, pasta gnocchi is, as the name suggests, similar in shape to potato gnocchi. If unavailable, use conchiglie or orecchiette.

Tomato and ricotta orecchiette

400 g (14 oz) orecchiette, or
   conchiglie or cavatelli
450 g (1 lb) Roma (plum) tomatoes
310 g (1¼ cups) ricotta cheese
40 g (1½ oz) Parmesan cheese,
   grated, plus extra, to serve
8 basil leaves, torn into pieces

Cook the pasta in a large saucepan of boiling salted water until *al dente*.

Score a cross in the top of each tomato, plunge them into boiling water (you can use the pasta water) for 20 seconds, then drain and peel the skin away from the cross. Core and chop the tomatoes. Mash the ricotta, then add the Parmesan and season with salt and freshly ground black pepper.

Drain the pasta and return to the pan. Add the ricotta mixture, the tomato and basil. Season and toss. Serve at once with Parmesan.

Serves 4

Tagliatelle with salmon and creamy dill dressing

350 g (12 oz) fresh tagliatelle
60 ml (¼ cup) olive oil
3 x 200 g (7 oz) salmon fillets, skinned
  and boned (ask your fishmonger to
  do this for you)
3 garlic cloves, crushed
375 ml (1½ cups) cream
1½ tablespoons chopped dill
1 teaspoon mustard powder
1 tablespoon lemon juice
35 g (⅓ cup) shaved Parmesan
  cheese

Cook the pasta in a large saucepan of boiling salted water until *al dente*. Drain, then toss with 1 tablespoon of the oil.

Meanwhile, heat the remaining oil in a large deep frying pan and cook the salmon for 2 minutes each side, or until crisp on the outside but still pink inside. Remove from the pan, cut into 2 cm (¾ inch) cubes and keep warm.

In the same pan, add the garlic and cook for 30 seconds, or until fragrant. Add the cream, dill and mustard powder, bring to the boil, then reduce the heat and simmer, stirring, for 4–5 minutes until thickened. Season.

Add the salmon and any juices, plus the lemon juice to the creamy dill sauce and stir until warmed through. Gently toss the sauce and salmon through the pasta and divide among four serving bowls. Sprinkle with the Parmesan and serve.

Serves 4

Pasta pronto

2 tablespoons extra virgin olive oil
4 garlic cloves, finely chopped
1 small red chilli, finely chopped
3 x 400 g (14 oz) cans crushed
  tomatoes
1 teaspoon sugar
80 ml (⅓ cup) dry white wine
3 tablespoons chopped herbs such
  as basil or parsley
400 g (14 oz) vermicelli (see Note)
35 g (⅓ cup) shaved Parmesan
  cheese

Heat the oil in a large deep frying pan and cook the garlic and chilli for 1 minute. Add the tomato, sugar, wine, herbs and 440 ml (1¾ cups) water. Bring to the boil and season.

Reduce the heat to medium and add the pasta, breaking the strands if they are too long. Cook for 10 minutes, or until the pasta is cooked, stirring often to stop the pasta from sticking. The pasta will thicken the sauce as it cooks. Season to taste and serve in bowls with shaved Parmesan.

Serves 4

Note: Vermicelli is a pasta similar to spaghetti, but thinner. You can also use spaghettini or angel hair pasta for this recipe.

Smoked salmon stracci in champagne sauce

375 g (13 oz) fresh stracci (see Notes)
1 tablespoon olive oil
2 large garlic cloves, crushed
125 ml (½ cup) champagne
250 ml (1 cup) thick (double/heavy)
  cream
200 g (7 oz) smoked salmon, cut into
  thin strips
2 tablespoons small capers in brine,
  rinsed and patted dry
2 tablespoons chopped chives
2 tablespoons chopped dill

Cook the pasta in a large saucepan of boiling salted water until *al dente*. Drain and return to the pan.

Meanwhile, heat the oil in a large frying pan and cook the garlic over medium heat for 30 seconds. Pour in the champagne and cook for 2–3 minutes, or until the liquid is reduced slightly. Add the cream and cook for 3–4 minutes, or until the sauce has thickened.

Add the sauce, salmon, capers and herbs to the hot pasta and toss gently. Season with salt and cracked black pepper and serve immediately.

Serves 4

Notes: Stracci is sold fresh and dried — either is suitable for this recipe — or you can use fresh or dried fettucine or tagliatelle.
Dried lasagne sheets can also be used instead of stracci. Break them into ragged pieces measuring about 8 x 13 cm (3 x 5 inches).